HOLIDAY CLUB
PROGRAMME
FOR 5- TO 11-YEAR OLDS

Scripture Union
207–209 Queensway,
Bletchley,
Milton Keynes
MK2 2EB
Email: info@scriptureunion.org.uk
Website: www.scriptureunion.org.uk

Scripture quotations are from the
Contemporary English Version published
by HarperCollins*Publishers* © 1991, 1992,
1995 American Bible Society or from the
Good News Bible, published by The Bible
Societies/HarperCollins Publishers Ltd, UK,
© American Bible Society, 1966, 1971,
1976, 1992.

'God is Love' copyright © 2011 Thank You
Music, adm. by Capital CMG Publishing
worldwide excl. UK & Europe, admin by
Integrity Music, part of the David C Cook
family, songs@integritymusic.com.

British Library Cataloguing-in-Publication Data
A catalogue record of this book is available
from the British Library.

Printed and bound in India by
Nutech Print Services

Cover and internal design: kwgraphicdesign

Main contributors: Maggie Barfield
and Gemma Willis
Additional material by Sarah Bingham,
Kay Morgan-Gurr, Bob Hartman, Alex Taylor
and Ro Willoughby

Scripture Union is an international Christian
charity working with churches in more than
130 countries.

Thank you for purchasing this book. Any profits
from this book support SU in England and
Wales to bring the good news of Jesus Christ
to children, young people and families and to
enable them to meet God through the Bible
and prayer.

Find out more about our work and how you
can get involved at:
• www.scriptureunion.org.uk
  (England and Wales)
• www.suscotland.org.uk (Scotland)
• www.suni.co.uk (Northern Ireland)
• www.scriptureunion.org (USA)
• www.su.org.au (Australia)

CONTENTS

INTRODUCTION

GUARDIANS OF ANCORA is a seven-day children's holiday club: an opening service, five (daily) club sessions and a closing service.

Once, the Hall of Memory in the city of Ancora was filled with wonderful story-treasures, each a reminder of one of the great stories of the Saga (the Bible). Now, many of those objects have been lost. Each day of the club, the task of the Guardians (the children at the club) will be to find a lost story-treasure, return it to the Hall of Memory and explore the story that it represents. As the Hall fills up, the Guardians will discover how each story fits together to reveal more about who Jesus is and how they might develop their own relationship with him.

The programme is devised from the faith-based app game **GUARDIANS OF ANCORA**. It can be run without any reference to the game, but you will find suggestions in each club session for using the game to complement the other activities.

GO TO >>>

- For **full details** of the aims, theme, setting and roles of GUARDIANS OF ANCORA, go to pages 8–20.
- For **general help** and hints on running a holiday club, go to page 21.
- For **outlines** for each day's session, go to page 35.
- For a **resource bank** of activity ideas, go to page 75.

MEETING JESUS

Service 1 Who is Jesus?
Matthew 16:13–16

Quest 1 Jesus calls the fishermen
Luke 5:1–11

Quest 2 Jesus heals the Roman officer's servant
Luke 7:1–10

Quest 3 Jesus heals a woman and a girl
Luke 8:40–56

Quest 4 Jesus heals a man who came through a roof
Luke 5:17–26

Quest 5 Jesus feeds 5,000
John 6:1–15,25–35

Service 2 Love the Lord!
Mark 12:28–34; Matthew 22:37

WHO IS IT FOR?

Every effort has been made to ensure this programme is suitable for children with little or no church background. It is a tool for churches whose desire is to reach out to children and their families outside their church community. It should work equally well for churches wishing to use it as a discipleship resource for children already part of the church family.

Hints and tips are given with each day's session for children who are new to a faith-based club, who are used to church, who have additional needs and who have backgrounds from other faiths.

GUARDIANS OF ANCORA RESOURCE BOOK

Packed with creative ideas on how to seek and discover stories that combine to give an overview of who Jesus is – ideas you can change and adapt to suit your club and context. There are also ideas for construction (craft), games, drama, creative prayer and worship. **GUARDIANS OF ANCORA** has a mixture of upfront presentation and small group activities, allowing children and leaders to build meaningful relationships with each other and with God.

Each Quest or daily session of **GUARDIANS OF ANCORA** is designed to work as an individual event, as well as forming part of a week-long club. If you have fewer days available, simply omit Quest 2 or 3.

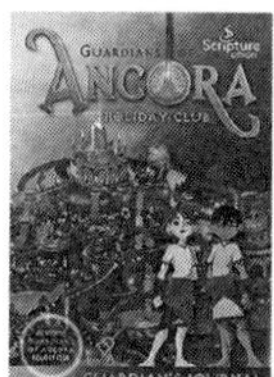

GUARDIAN'S JOURNAL FOR 8 TO 11S

This 48-page booklet contains all the key Bible text taken from the Contemporary English Version, along with small-group material, puzzles and extra information. It is ideal for use with 8 to 11s.

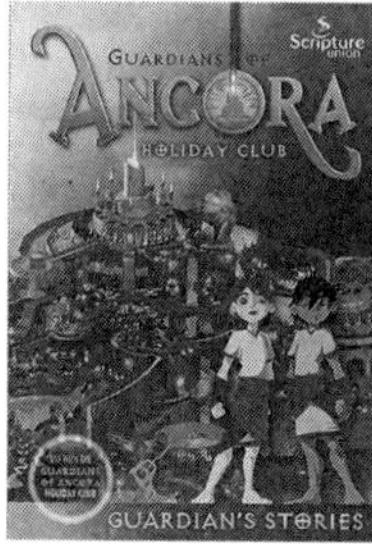

GUARDIAN'S STORIES FOR 5 TO 8S

This 32-page booklet contains retold Bible stories, with key Bible verses taken from the Contemporary English Version, along with small-group material, puzzles and extra information, for younger children.

There are hints and tips for using both these resources as part of the small-group time in each day's Quest. Both *Guardian's Journal* and *Guardian's Stories* help maintain contact with children's homes and act as a reminder, in the weeks after the club, of what the children experienced at **GUARDIANS OF ANCORA**. You can buy *Guardian's Journal* or *Guardian's Stories* as multiple copies – see the inside front cover for details.

GUARDIANS OF ANCORA MULTIMEDIA DOWNLOADS

To supplement your club a wealth of multimedia downloadable resources are available from the **GUARDIANS OF ANCORA** multimedia downloads area.

Resources include:
⊕ video retellings of the Bible stories in each Quest
⊕ **GUARDIANS OF ANCORA** theme song
⊕ printable versions of the photocopiable resources
⊕ drama and story scripts
⊕ administration forms
⊕ a parallel programme for under-5s, following the same Bible passages and themes as the main programme
⊕ a parallel programme for 11 to 14s, following the same Bible passages and themes as the main programme
⊕ a training course for young leaders aged 14 to 18 (Apprentice Elders)
⊕ training sessions for your team
⊕ ideas to involve families and friends of those at the club
⊕ logos, posters...

... and more!

You can also read about other people's experiences and check out the advice given by other users on the message boards.

GUARDIANS OF ANCORA THEME SONG

'We are the **GUARDIANS OF ANCORA**' is the **GUARDIANS OF ANCORA** holiday club theme song.

For theme song lyrics and sheet music, go to page 106. For these plus an MP3 of the song go to the **GUARDIANS OF ANCORA** multimedia downloads area.

LEARN AND REMEMBER SONG

'God is Love' (Nick and Becky Drake) will help the children to learn the **GUARDIANS OF ANCORA** *Learn and remember* verse: Matthew 22:37. An MP3 of the song is available to download from iTunes.

For *Learn and remember* song lyrics and sheet music, go to page 111.

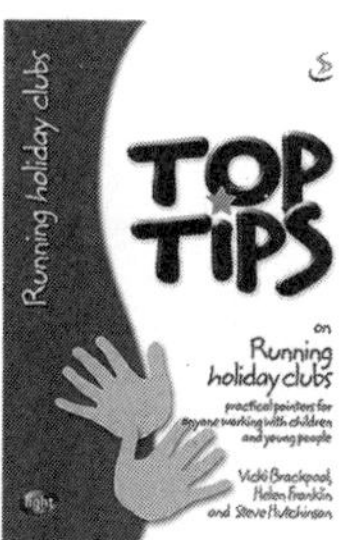

TOP TIPS ON RUNNING HOLIDAY CLUBS

Practical advice and real-life experience to help you run a Bible-based holiday club, with suggestions to inspire and help you grow your team.

PUBLICITY MATERIALS AND MERCHANDISE

See the inside back cover for details of the publicity materials produced by Christian Publicity and Outreach. (Please note, CPO resources are not available through Scripture Union.)

GUARDIANS OF ANCORA APP

There's a whole virtual world waiting to be explored within the free-to-play children's app **GUARDIANS OF ANCORA**. Each session in the resource book contains suggestions for how to use the app in the club and at home.

Go to your app store and search for '**GUARDIANS OF ANCORA**'.

CHECKLIST

Which resources will you need to run your club and how many of each?

	Quantity
GUARDIANS OF ANCORA resource book	
Guardian's Journal **Single copy**	
10-pack	
Guardian's Stories **Single copy**	
10-pack	
GUARDIANS OF ANCORA downloads	
Theme song MP3	
Learn and remember song MP3	
Training video downloads	
Top Tips on Running Holiday Clubs	
Remember to visit the **GUARDIANS OF ANCORA** multimedia downloads area and download:	
all documents as a Zip file	✓
your choice of documents	✓

THE BASICS

THE BASICS I
AIMS AND BIBLE PROGRAMME

WHAT ARE *YOUR* AIMS?

The aims of the **GUARDIANS OF ANCORA** holiday club are below, but each individual club will have its own specific aims, too. **GUARDIANS OF ANCORA** can provide a manageable, creative and fun way of reaching out to the children of your neighbourhood with the welcoming love of Jesus. It can provide an excellent opportunity to blow any misconceptions away about God and the Bible and show that following Jesus can be a great adventure.

You are likely to be focusing on the days or week of your club, but remember that the holiday club is not an isolated event. Where does it fit into your plans for children's work and with the church's ongoing evangelism and discipleship programme? How might you build on this to draw children further into church life (not necessarily or only through Sunday worship)? What opportunities will the club offer for your church to be more involved with the local community or to create and sustain links with schools in your area?

WORKING OUT YOUR AIMS
⊕ Make a copy of page 95 or print it from the **GUARDIANS OF ANCORA** multimedia downloads area.
⊕ Cut the page into strips.
⊕ Cut some blank strips as well.
⊕ Get together with others, including your church leaders and holiday club team.
⊕ Write your own aims on the blank strips.
⊕ Mix all the strips together.

What do you want your holiday club to achieve, in your situation?
⊕ As a group, sort the aims into your order of priority.
⊕ Pick out the top aims (a maximum of three) and make sure all the team know them.

Plan to evaluate **GUARDIANS OF ANCORA** after the event to see if you met your aims.
⊕ Decide now how you'll do that.
⊕ How will you measure success?

Go to the **GUARDIANS OF ANCORA** multimedia download area to download a form to assess how you met your aims.

THE AIMS OF GUARDIANS OF ANCORA

Through seven stories, from the New Testament, the **GUARDIANS OF ANCORA** programme looks at who Jesus is. It reveals that God had a plan in sending Jesus to earth – to restore humanity to relationship with him. It builds, day on day, helping children form an overview of the things that Jesus did and demonstrating the power of faith in Christ. It gives children the option to consider their own relationship with God and how this might impact their lives. Children are invited to consider the stories they hear about Jesus as treasure – stories that are of immense value and importance. As they seek the treasure of these stories, they will be encouraged to seek and find their own place in God's big, ongoing, forever story.

AIMS

- ⊕ To help children understand who Jesus is.
- ⊕ To invite children to recognise their place in God's story by becoming lifelong followers of Jesus, and to enable children who are already in a relationship with him to grow in their faith and understanding.
- ⊕ To create lasting positive memories of Christian community, to build relationships and help children and their families become part of a church community.
- ⊕ To offer a safe and fun environment for all the children.
- ⊕ To encourage the growth of Christian faith in all the adults who are involved in the club, whether team members or parents/carers who may be on the premises for the very first time.

THE GUARDIANS OF ANCORA BIBLE PROGRAMME

The services begin with an exploration of who Jesus is and conclude with the amazing invitation to 'Love the Lord your God with all your heart, soul and mind' (Matthew 22:37). Between these two worship events are the five Bible stories of the club sessions, spanning much of Jesus' ministry.

PRESENTING THE BIBLE STORY

GUARDIANS OF ANCORA equips you to tell the Bible story in several ways:
- ⊕ You may have a gifted storyteller on your team: encourage them to use their skills and bring the Bible passages to life, in their own way.

- ⊕ The **GUARDIANS OF ANCORA** multimedia download area has a video story episode for each Quest: use it to tell the story or to reinforce your own storytelling, in a different way.
- ⊕ Each Quest includes story headlines that can be developed into a retold story.
- ⊕ There are full scripts for reading aloud in the Treasure Store (page 76) and in the **GUARDIANS OF ANCORA** multimedia download area.

Whichever way you choose to tell the Bible story, be sure to make the storytelling a distinctive event in your programme: this is the moment when the story behind the story-treasure is revealed to the Guardians! Aim to make it as memorable and exhilarating as you can!

BIBLE REFERENCES, STORYLINES AND AIMS: DAY BY DAY

SERVICE I
WHO IS JESUS?

KEY PASSAGES
Matthew 16:13–16,21; John 3:16

KEY STORYLINES
- ⊕ A Guardian finds several small bags each with a large luggage label attached with a name on it in big letters. Each name is followed by a large question mark. This helps to introduce the theme of wondering who Jesus is.
- ⊕ God sends Jesus to earth to show people how much he loves them and to enable them to be in relationship with him once more.
- ⊕ When Jesus starts to do amazing things, people begin to realise who he is – the long-awaited Messiah, Redeemer and Saviour.

KEY AIMS
- ⊕ To set the scene for the holiday club, explaining who Jesus is and preparing the children to discover God's plan to restore his relationship with humanity.
- ⊕ To launch the holiday club so that church members can commit to pray for the coming week.
- ⊕ To welcome any children and their associated adults coming to the club who are not usually part of the worshipping community.

QUEST I
JESUS CALLS THE FISHERMEN

KEY PASSAGE
Luke 5:1–11

KEY STORYLINES
⊕ The Guardians find a pile of fishing nets, which open up the story of the call of the fishermen.
⊕ By listening to Jesus the fishermen are able to catch very large numbers of fish, when without him they had worked hard, but caught nothing.
⊕ Jesus asks the fishermen to leave their homes and fish for people instead of fish. He calls them to follow him.

KEY AIMS
⊕ To welcome each child to the club, setting the tone for the next few days.
⊕ To find out that, just as Jesus called the fishermen to follow him, he calls us too.
⊕ To understand that following Jesus is sometimes costly, but always brings blessing.
⊕ To regard and treat these stories as wonderful treasure

QUEST II
JESUS HEALS THE ROMAN OFFICER'S SERVANT

KEY PASSAGE
Luke 7:1–10

KEY STORYLINES
⊕ The Guardians find a pair of Roman sandals, which launch the story of the Roman officer's servant.
⊕ The Roman officer's servant is extremely unwell and about to die. The officer demonstrates great faith in Jesus and his servant is healed.
⊕ Faith in Jesus, his authority and power is all that is needed for the servant to be healed.

KEY AIMS
⊕ To welcome each child to the club and remind them of what has happened so far.
⊕ To find out that Jesus is God's Son and has his authority and power.
⊕ To identify that having faith in Jesus can have amazing results.
⊕ To have a growing sense of excitement and wonder about finding the story-treasures.

QUEST III
JESUS HEALS A WOMAN AND A GIRL

KEY PASSAGE
Luke 8:40–56

KEY STORYLINES
⊕ The Guardians find a collection of handprints, which release the story of Jairus' daughter and the woman who touched Jesus' coat.
⊕ The woman who touched Jesus' coat has been unwell for 12 years and no one has been able to heal her. Her faith in Jesus combined with his power to heal means that only one touch of his coat is enough to restore her to health.
⊕ The people claim that Jairus' daughter is dead, but Jesus is able to restore her to life.

KEY AIMS
⊕ To welcome each child to the club and remind them of everything that has happened so far.
⊕ To find out that even though Jesus is very powerful he is still interested in the detail of our lives.
⊕ To understand that Jesus has great compassion on those who are unwell or in need, and that he calls those who follow him to have the same compassion.
⊕ To create a mood of anticipation about Quest 4, in which Jesus performs another exciting miracle and reveals a little more of who he is.

QUEST IV
JESUS HEALS A MAN WHO CAME THROUGH A ROOF!

KEY PASSAGE
Luke 5:17–26

KEY STORYLINES
⊕ The Guardians unwrap a selection of random objects, the last of which is a mat, leading them to the story of Jesus healing a man who comes to him through a hole in a roof!
⊕ A paralysed man is brought to Jesus, but because there is no space for the men carrying him to get through the crowds they climb onto the roof of the building where Jesus is teaching and lower the man through the ceiling.
⊕ On seeing the faith of these men, Jesus heals the paralysed man.

KEY AIMS
⊕ To understand that God has the power to heal and restore.
⊕ To identify that in each of the healing miracles explored so far Jesus comments on the faith of the people involved.
⊕ To realise that part of being healed and restored is being forgiven, and that Jesus has the power to forgive our sins.
⊕ To grasp what it means to put faith in Jesus day to day.

QUEST V
JESUS FEEDS 5,000

KEY PASSAGES
John 6:1–15,25–35

KEY STORYLINES
⊕ The Guardians find tins of tuna and bread rolls, which reveal the story of Jesus feeding 5,000 people.
⊕ A crowd of people who have seen Jesus perform miracles and heal the sick are following him, eager to find out more about him.
⊕ Jesus takes two small fish and five loaves from a young boy and miraculously multiplies the food to feed the entire crowd, with twelve full baskets of leftovers.

KEY AIMS
⊕ To welcome each child to the club and to give them a memorable final day.
⊕ To discover that Jesus is able to use what we have to great effect when we allow him to do so.
⊕ To understand what Jesus means when he describes himself as 'the bread of life'.
⊕ To consider what it means to have a personal relationship with Jesus and to respond.

SERVICE II
LOVE THE LORD!

KEY PASSAGES
Mark 12:28–34; Matthew 22:37

KEY STORYLINES
⊕ Two volunteer Guardians find five balloons, which remind us of how important it is to love God with all that we are and have.
⊕ Jesus has shown us how much he loves us and he invites us to love him in return. Part of loving Jesus is showing his love to others.
⊕ Loving God should impact every area of our lives – our hearts, minds and strength – as the Guardians will have memorised in their *Learn and remember* verse.

KEY AIMS
⊕ To be excited about loving Jesus and following him.
⊕ To recognise Jesus' love for us and his call for us to love others.
⊕ To share with the rest of the church family what has been happening in the holiday club.
⊕ To welcome any children and their associated adults who have been part of the club but do not usually come to a service.
⊕ To be confident that the treasures of these stories will continue to be with us, even now the holiday club is over.

A **SHORTER** HOLIDAY CLUB PROGRAMME

If you have less time, Quests 2 and/or 3 can be omitted.

The message of who Jesus is, his love for his people and God's ultimate plan of salvation will still be central to the programme, with the children hearing how Jesus calls us to follow him, challenges us to put our faith in him and will use all that we have to do amazing things, if we let him. Children will also be invited to consider their own response to Jesus.

GO TO >>>

⊕ For a Bob Hartman download about storytelling, go to the **GUARDIANS OF ANCORA** multimedia download area.

⊕ For the daily sessions (**Quests**) go to page 35.

⊕ To **plan** what needs to be done and when, go to page 31.

⊕ For **details** of the theme, setting and team roles, read on.

THE BASICS II
THEMES AND SETTINGS

ALL ABOUT ANCORA

ANCORA, the City of Hope, is built on a hill next to the sea. At the summit stands the Spire of Light which lights up the whole city. The stories of the Saga (the Bible) are told here every day, and the power of storytelling fuels the light of the Spire. Each Story of the Saga is represented by a story-treasure (some sort of object or artefact): these are stored in the **Hall of Memory**, the central setting for the GUARDIANS OF ANCORA holiday club.

Many of these story-treasures are missing and the people of Ancora are determined to get them back so they can, once again, tell the stories that have been lost. The existing Guardians have recovered some of these but others still need to be found and so they have sent out an appeal for new recruits. The GUARDIANS OF ANCORA holiday club picks up the theme at this point.

The biblical material and the setting link together naturally: the holiday club is about helping children discover the story of Jesus, God's Saviour, and develop their own relationship with him.

It's really up to you how closely and deeply you identify your club with the world of Ancora. But you can be confident that the children will relish using their imaginations and 'become' part of the setting you create.

PEOPLE OF ANCORA

The Keeper of the Keys and **Kal**, the Aquaneer are the two upfront presenters who hold the programme together and lead the search for each day's story-treasure. The Keeper is one of the most important people in the city, as she holds together all the official memories, story-treasures and learning that make up the story of the city. Kal is responsible for all the waterways of the city including the great aquavators, which move boats around the different levels of the city.

As **Guardians**, the children are on Quests to find the lost story-treasures, hear the stories of Jesus and learn who Jesus is and how they might develop their own relationship with him. They are in **Companies** (six to eight children per Company), and each Company is led by an **Elder Guardian**, who may be helped by one or more **Apprentice Elders**. They and everyone else at the club are members of **The Guild** of Ancora.

Fabula spends most of her time telling the stories of the Saga, and from her the children will hear the Bible stories. **The Shiner** is an extra upfront presenter – he is friendly, unconventional and slightly unpredictable.

Head of **The Guild** and chief citizen of Ancora is the **Guildmaster**. In your club, this is the person who is the overall leader and organiser, but probably not an upfront presenter.

More detailed character profiles are available from the GUARDIANS OF ANCORA multimedia downloads area.

PLACES OF ANCORA

The Hall of Memory is the main setting for the holiday club and is the most exciting library-museum-gallery in the world. It houses books, films, music, games, story-treasures and more.

The **Theatre of the Saga** is where stories of the Saga (Bible stories) are told. The telling acts as a power source, fuelling the **Spire of Light**, which gets brighter the more stories are told.

FIREBUGS

Firebugs are small insects that:
⊕ provide light
⊕ help Guardians find their way
⊕ may be used as a form of currency: Guardians may need to trade as they go on their quests.

Photocopiable firebugs are available on page 97, and should be copied onto a different colour of paper for each club day. Give each child a firebug as they arrive at the club; hand out extra firebugs for answering questions, participating in activities and anything else you can think of!

SETTING UP **YOUR** VENUE

THE BEST PLACE TO MEET

Choosing the right venue is very important. Sometimes a community hall or school is a well-equipped, neutral venue that can be non-threatening for children and parents outside the church. However, you may wish to use this opportunity to introduce children and parents to your church building. This can also help save on the cost of hiring an alternative venue. The venue needs to have enough space for the number of children and the type of activities you are planning. You will need access to the venue before the holiday club to ensure necessary preparations can be made.

For more advice on choosing a venue and adult:child ratios go to the **GUARDIANS OF ANCORA** multimedia downloads area and download 'Legal requirements for holiday clubs'.

SETTING UP THE ROOM

If you have the space and can leave your room set up, from day to day, there are many ways to transform your club space into a Hall of Memory. The setting of a fabulous museum-library-gallery gives wide scope for decorating the meeting space: great display cases for the treasures; bookcases; giant screens (TVs or projector screens); giant drawers with plans and papers spilling out; maps and charts; large pictures of biblical characters; 'portraits' of the team in baroque frames (pasta shapes stuck on board and sprayed gold); a quiet area in a tent-style gazebo; and so on. Experiment with a projector (even an old overhead one) to project photos of elaborate libraries on the walls or floor, especially as children arrive for the club. You can find amazing photos on sites such as Pinterest.

All this will help to spark children's imaginations. Think creatively how you can transform your venue into an exciting place.

If you cannot leave your room set up from day to day, prepare pictures on display boards or large banners that can be put into place quickly at the start of each session. Make sure you allow extra time for this and have team members lined up to help.

FIREBUGS

String fairy lights, high enough in the room to be convincing as firebugs, lighting the Hall of Memory (follow the safety instructions on the packaging).

FILL THE SCREEN

If you are using a video projector or OHP to project the song words, for example, use interesting images when it is not being used, so that the screen is never blank. Find the **GUARDIANS OF ANCORA** logo and other themed artwork in the **GUARDIANS OF ANCORA** multimedia downloads area.

EXTRA ROOMS

If you have more than one room, think carefully about which activities to site in which part of the venue. You need easy routes between rooms and to minimise 'shuffle time' between different parts of your timetable.

If you have multiple rooms, appoint someone (maybe an Apprentice Elder) to be the 'herald' each day. This person will remind groups in distant venues about the time, take messages for the Guildmaster and generally help get everyone to the right place at the right time.

VENUE MAPS

Once you have decided the locations within your venue, give each team member a map to remind them of what is happening where – and so they can work out where they need to be, at any given time in the session. Include emergency exits, toilets and 'no entry' areas on the map, too.

SPACES, WITHIN THE VENUE

UPFRONT PRESENTATION

The holiday club will be greatly enhanced if the area (a stage, if possible) where the upfront presentation takes place can be transformed into part of the Hall of Memory. This is where the Keeper of the Keys and Kal will run the programme. The boundary for the stage area can be marked by a masking tape line across the floor.

STORY SPACE

Designate part of the room to be the amphitheatre with a place for the storyteller. (It need not be in a different room but, for instance, the children could turn and face a different way when it comes to the story time.)

DRAMA

Think about where you will present the daily drama. This is probably not your main presentation area as the scenery will need to change for each drama episode. A raised stage is ideal to allow all the children to see the action.

BAND

Position The Firebugs carefully; they are likely to come with large amounts of equipment and need access to electricity. Leave space for the stage to be used for other things, too! Keep the children away from this area and make sure that routes around the building do not require them to step over cables, and so on.

SCREEN(S) AND PROJECTOR

Work out where to locate the projection screen, for projecting song words, club logo and so on; and where to position the projector so it does not obstruct the children's view or become a hazard.

'GREEN ROOM'

A draped-off area or a linking room will be useful for the drama team to emerge from. This can double as a 'staff room' for team members.

COMPANIES

The rest of the room can be divided into a space for each Company. Remember, each Company will include adult Elder Guardians and six to eight children, both Guardians and Apprentice Elders.

Much will depend on whether the areas can be left from day to day. Larger space could mean the Company areas can become more elaborate as the week progresses, with the Ancora map, banners and flags, firebugs, collections of things the children have found or made and areas for sitting and working.

THE BASICS III
TEAM ROLES AND TASKS

These pages will take you through all the roles and functions that will help your club run smoothly. Not all have to happen at the holiday club or all the time the club is running so individuals may take on several roles and functions.

The holiday club (and those taking part) will thrive when there are a variety of support teams and when individuals take responsibility for different areas of the programme. If you are running a holiday club for the first time and only have a small team of volunteers you may not be able to fill all these roles or teams. So, we have noted which roles we see as essential (indicating some extra tasks those people will need to take on) and those that are great to have, if you are blessed with a larger team.

Possible roles are listed in the table on pages 16 and 17 with space for you to write in the name(s) of the team members. Remember – these are the roles, the different tasks that people may do. You do not need a different person for each role – and many roles are optional, the club will still work without them. Team roles and tasks are explained in more detail on pages 15–20.

Job descriptions for each role are available at the **GUARDIANS OF ANCORA** multimedia downloads area.

Print these out for each person on the team to help everyone know how they fit into the whole club. (Some people may have several job descriptions.) Use the reverse side of the sheet to remind them of specific details of your holiday club such as dates, times, your club aims, training workshops and so on.

It is possible (though very hard work!) to run a holiday club with a minimum team of three adult leaders. The larger and more experienced your team, the more options and activities you can offer, but don't be put off by small numbers. Work and adapt with what you've got.

TEAM ROLES AND FUNCTIONS SUMMARY

The table on pages 16 and 17 overleaf shows all the roles you may choose to use in your holiday club: some are optional and others can be combined.

TEAM ROLES AND FUNCTIONS IN DETAIL

CORE PLANNING TEAM

All the helpers should be involved in planning and preparing for **GUARDIANS OF ANCORA**, but you will need a smaller team to coordinate things and make some initial decisions. As well as the holiday club's overall leader, this should include your most experienced leaders, your minister and your children's workers.

GUILDMASTER OR WARDEN OF THE GUILD THE OVERALL HOLIDAY CLUB LEADER

The overall leader and coordinator is ideally someone who is not involved in the presentation. Their role is to:
⊕ lead the planning of the holiday club, before and during the event
⊕ make any on-the-spot decisions, such as accepting extra children at the door
⊕ keep the whole programme to time, moving things on when necessary
⊕ look at quality of presentation, watching out for problems such as too much drifting off the timetable
⊕ watch out for children who are not joining in well and help them to become part of things
⊕ be the person to whom everyone would report in the event of a fire
⊕ liaise with parents and carers
⊕ be a PR figure.

TEAM ROLES AND FUNCTIONS

ROLE	FUNCTION	ESSENTIAL/ OPTIONAL	UPFRONT/BEHIND THE SCENES
Core planning team	Small group to lead organising the club	Essential	Behind the scenes
Guildmaster or Warden of the Guild	Overall leader of the holiday club	Essential	Both
Keeper of the Keys	Co-presenter (main)	Essential	Upfront
Kal, the Aquaneer	Co-presenter (main)	Essential	Upfront
Fabula or Fabler	Storyteller	Optional (this role could be a shared one)	Upfront
The Shiner, an expert in talking to firebugs!	Another presenter	Optional	Upfront
Elder Guardians	Small group leaders	Essential	A bit of both
Apprentice Elders	Junior leaders or helpers	Optional	A bit of both
Registration coordinator and team	Books children in; keeps records	Essential	Both
The Firebugs	Live worship band	Optional	Upfront
Drama leader	Recruits drama team; runs daily drama	Optional	Both
Games coordinator	Organises all games activities at the club	Optional	Either or both
Construction/craft organiser	Organises hands-on creative activities	Optional	Either or both
Refreshment person or team	Makes sure refreshments happen on time and safely	Essential	Behind the scenes
First-aider	As required; maintains records	Preferable	Behind the scenes
Technical manager	Makes sure everything works as and when it should	Optional, depending on what you are using	Behind the scenes
Publicity and admin person or team	Publicise the club; club paperwork	Optional	Behind the scenes
Health and safety person	Ensures safety of everyone at the club	Optional	Behind the scenes
Meeters and greeters	Available to chat to adults as they bring and collect their children	Optional	A bit of both
Prayer team	Prays	Essential	Behind the scenes

SPECIAL SKILLS	TEAM MEMBER
Organisation, monitoring, leading	
Confident, able to engage and involve children	
Confident, able to engage and involve children	
Communication	
Acting and imagination	
Leading small groups of children	
Willing to learn and join in	
Attention to detail, welcoming and friendly	
Musical; leading worship	
Acting and team leading	
Energy and enthusiasm	
Creativity and patience	
Organisation and planning	
Current first-aid qualification	
Practical and technical	
Risk assessments	
Welcoming, friendly and reassuring	

THE KEEPER OF THE KEYS AND KAL, THE AQUANEER THE MAIN UPFRONT PRESENTERS

The main presenters of **GUARDIANS OF ANCORA**. Together, they guide children through the session, introducing the different elements and delivering some of the teaching for the day.

They should be confident in their roles upfront and have experience of leading a programme in a fun but flexible manner. They need to keep the programme moving and engage with the children.

FABULA OR FABLER THE STORYTELLER

Each day, the Bible story is told or introduced by the chief storyteller, using scripts and suggestions for visual aids. Fabula may tell the story or introduce another storyteller. The person telling the story needs to be a confident and skilled communicator. They need to prepare the story thoroughly and be happy telling it to a group of children.

THE SHINER A PRESENTER

The Shiner is a quirky character who adds an element of humour and – sometimes – confusion to the club. Look for a team member who is a natural joker and who can work spontaneously with the main presenters and take on some of the upfront tasks. This optional role will add extra fun to proceedings, with the right person in the part.

ELDER GUARDIANS AND APPRENTICE ELDERS

These are the leaders of each Company (small group) and those helping them. The Elder Guardian has responsibility for the Guardians (children) in the Company and will also be supporting the Apprentice Elders, who may never have been involved in a holiday club before or may be someone who could be a leader at next year's club.

ELDER GUARDIAN

The small group Guardian should be at the club every day and will be the person with whom the children have the most personal contact. The leader's role is to get to know the children so that they feel welcome and comfortable at **GUARDIANS OF ANCORA**. The programme is designed to give these leaders enough time in the Companies to have meaningful discussions, including ones that apply the teaching programme to the children's lives.

They should coordinate all small-group activities and sit with the children in their Companies during the upfront times. They should have a copy of the register and be aware of any special needs and food allergies, ensuring that children all leave safely at the end of the day's session.

If you have a large holiday club, you may appoint someone to coordinate six or eight Companies whose Guardians are all in one age range. It is best if these coordinators do not have a group of their own.

APPRENTICE ELDERS

The role of the Apprentice Elder is to support the Elder Guardian, and ideally they should also be available every day. This is a good way to develop the leadership skills of young or inexperienced team members.

Under-18s count as children, when you're working out adult:child ratios. If you have a lot of Apprentice Elders helping in Companies, you will need *more* Elder Guardians, rather than fewer.

All team members should be given training in dealing with children, especially in relation to physical contact and not being with children alone out of sight of others, but Elder Guardians and Apprentice Elders especially need to be aware of child protection issues and policies.

THINK ABOUT >>>

New to running a holiday club? Or new team members this time?

More experienced but wanting to work on aspects like storytelling or leading small groups?

Even if your team members already work with children in the church, the shared experience of training together will benefit all of you!

Go to the **GUARDIANS OF ANCORA** multimedia downloads area for training modules on a whole range of topics and skills that will build your confidence as leaders.

REGISTRATION COORDINATOR
(AND TEAM)

Responsible for:
- allocating children to Companies
- checking children in and out each day
- checking forms are completed fully
- making a register, based on names and ages
- giving a copy of the register to the Elder Guardian of each Company
- keeping a check on team sizes if more children register during **GUARDIANS OF ANCORA**.
- ensuring each child is to be picked up or has permission to walk home themselves. If you have a lot of children attending the club, it can be hard to keep track of who has permission to collect which child, especially when parents help each other out. A collection slip, which can be given to the adult who will pick the child up, is on the **GUARDIANS OF ANCORA** multimedia downloads area.

FORWARD PLANNING

If possible, encourage parents of children to complete booking forms in advance to be returned to the leader of the holiday club, school office or community group leader. This means you can allocate children to groups in advance and you will already be aware of dietary requirements, medical issues and physical, educational or behavioural special needs. Remember to check these when planning the club activities!

'ON THE DAY' REGISTRATION

In some contexts, pre-registering is not practical: ensure on the first day that there are plenty of extra volunteers available to help greet the children and their parents or carers and to provide them with the registration form to fill in. Children should not attend the event if permission has not been granted. As this can be a lengthy process, you should open the doors earlier on the first day. If the registration process is extended, engage the children in parachute games, upfront games or a short film.

IDENTIFICATION

- Each team member should have an appropriate, clearly labelled badge to identify them and their role.
- The children registered for **GUARDIANS OF ANCORA** should each have their own badge, which should be taken off before they leave the club.
- Any adult or child on site not wearing an appropriate badge should be challenged.
- Each child can be given a new sticky-backed badge each day, when they register. (Parents may not like their children to wear pin badges since they can be sharp and can damage clothes.)

THE FIREBUGS

Name your live music group after the friendly insects that light the city and the pathways for quests.

Having a live band can add something special to a holiday club. The band could be creatively dressed with antenna headbands, giant spectacles and clip-on wings!

If you can't use live music, then sing along to a CD. You could also consider having a group of dancers instead, who lead everyone in actions to songs, either with existing actions or their own.

DRAMA LEADER (AND TEAM)

The drama team needs a leader to recruit a team of five to ten actors who are reasonably confident and have the ability to project their voices, and coordinate rehearsals. They should appoint one of the drama team to collect and prepare the costumes and props. The drama team members should be willing to learn their lines and to practise each sketch until they can perform it with confidence.

GAMES COORDINATOR

This person needs to:

- ⊕ consider what games to play, based on the number of children, your venue and equipment available
- ⊕ take responsibility for ensuring all the games equipment is in the correct place at the right time
- ⊕ plan for bad-weather alternatives, if you are hoping to be outside for games
- ⊕ explain how to play each game
- ⊕ supervise the activity, if required.

CONSTRUCTION/CRAFT ORGANISER

This person need to:

- ⊕ acquire materials and equipment beforehand (ask people for specific items, go shopping, visit a local scrapstore)
- ⊕ take responsibility for ensuring all the equipment needed for the construction, creative prayer and Company activities is in the correct places at the right time
- ⊕ get as much as possible of the craft preparations done in advance (there may well be church members who can't help at the club but will be happy to help with cutting out, shopping and so on)
- ⊕ prepare a finished version of each item to show the children what they are making
- ⊕ be able to explain how the item is made.

THINK ABOUT >>>

A group of people to source the necessary materials will be invaluable, especially in the run-up to **GUARDIANS OF ANCORA**. They can make templates and patterns for children to draw around or cut out, help produce prototypes of each design and pass on any hints to the Elder Guardians.

Involve local schools in amassing reusable material to use during the week (such as yogurt pots, glass jars, plastic bottles, travel magazines for collage). This actively involves people in contributing to the club before it has begun, including the children, and alerts the school to the club's existence, bringing extra publicity.

REFRESHMENT PERSON OR TEAM

This person and team will play a vital role during the club times. They will be responsible for:

- ⊕ checking with the registration team that you have no children with food allergies
- ⊕ obtaining and preparing the refreshments for the children at the agreed time
- ⊕ being sensitive to faith-related food laws
- ⊕ tidying up after the refreshments have been given out.

If you are providing anything more than a drink and a biscuit, you should have someone with a food hygiene certificate. Think about using (recyclable) disposable cups or bottles to save on washing-up time.

FIRST-AIDER

Aim to have at least one member of your team with a valid first-aid certificate. If possible have assistants too – a male for the boys and a female for the girls. These people will need a current first-aid certificate and access to a first-aid kit. You will also need an accident book to record any incidents or accidents. (This is essential in the event of any insurance claim. A record of the matter should be noted, along with details of action taken. It should be countersigned where appropriate.)

TECHNICAL MANAGER

The amount of technology used will vary with the size and nature of each club, but these days it is hard to manage without some technical equipment. A technical manager could take responsibility for setting up and running:

- ⊕ Visual – laptop and projector, or OHP; screen, or DVD and TV.
- ⊕ Audio – PA for presenters and band; CD/MP3 player.

PUBLICITY AND CLUB ADMIN PERSON OR TEAM

A computer-literate person, or team of people, should take responsibility for all the design, printing and publicity for **GUARDIANS OF ANCORA**. Your aim should be to produce publicity that is visually impressive, consistent, accurate and attractive.

For more ideas about publicity and club administration paperwork, before, during and after **GUARDIANS OF ANCORA**, go to page 27.

HEALTH AND SAFETY PERSON

The person in charge of health and safety will be responsible for ensuring that no child leaves the building unless they have permission to do so, and that only children or adults who are part of **GUARDIANS OF ANCORA** are allowed to enter the building or area set aside for the club.

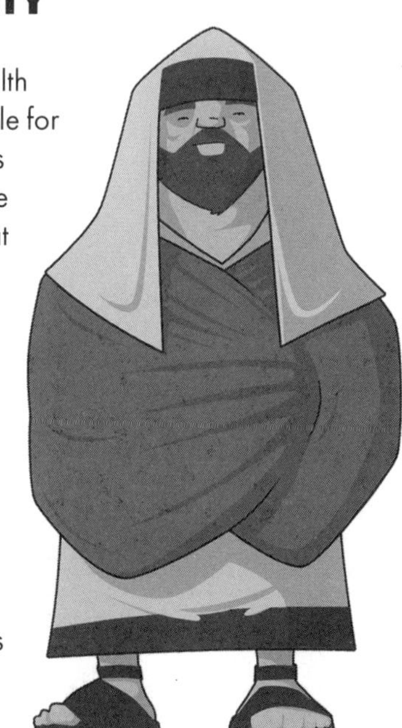

Duties and responsibilities of the health and safety person are listed further in Basics 5: Legal requirements on page 30.

MEETERS AND GREETERS

It's not essential, but it can be a real bonus to have people 'hanging around' to chat with adults, as they bring or collect their children. You might like to invite church staff to be part of this informal team, especially if they are not helping run the club: it is a good opportunity to start getting to know people. It is particularly useful to have extra helpers on the first day.

PRAYER TEAM

Make sure you have a team of people committed to pray throughout the preparation and the club itself. Keep the whole church well informed too.

The prayer team should keep on praying for the children in the club in the months after **GUARDIANS OF ANCORA**.

DEVELOPING PEOPLE'S POTENTIAL

As well as being a time of great fun and development for the children attending, a holiday club is also an important time for the adults leading and helping out. Helping with a holiday club can be a big step for people in the development of their gifts and ministry.

HOW DOES A HOLIDAY CLUB DEVELOP PEOPLE'S POTENTIAL?

- ⊕ It involves people in the church who don't usually work with children.
- ⊕ It is an opportunity for people of all ages to work together in a way that may not happen at any other time of the year. (A regular comment at one holiday club from team members is, 'This is the best week of the year in church!' It's probably the most demanding and tiring too!)
- ⊕ It develops people's gifts and lets them take risks.
- ⊕ It discovers people's untapped gifts and enthusiasms. For example, you may have online gamers in your congregation!
- ⊕ It provides a structure for the overall leadership of the club or church to seek out and encourage people to 'have a go'. Look at who you have available and ask people personally, giving them good reasons why you think they could fulfil whatever task you have identified. This suggests that you believe in them and they are far more likely to agree to get involved!

THE BASICS IV
PLANNING YOUR PROGRAMME

THE **SERVICES**

GUARDIANS OF ANCORA includes two services for all-age worship, one to start the club and one to finish. These are designed to be an integral part of the club. As an opener for the club, the first service will have a clear aim and motivate the children to want to attend. (Children who don't attend this first service will still find it easy to join the club on the first day, though!)

These give you a natural connection to encourage children from outside your church community and their families into a church service. Research shows that if you advertise the club as including the services (so, a seven-day programme rather than a five-day one), children and families with little or no church background are more likely to attend.

The services could be at the same time as your usual Sunday service, or on a different day or at a different time.

GO TO >>>

⊕ The all-age service for the start of the holiday club is on pages 36–39.

⊕ The all-age service for the end of the holiday club is on pages 71–74.

THE DAILY **QUESTS**

The daily Quests in **GUARDIANS OF ANCORA** follow a regular pattern that has been popular with many groups, but you don't have to follow this pattern! Plan your programme for your club!

⊕ Decide on the mix of all together and small group time that will work well with your venue, timing and numbers.
⊕ Select which programme elements are most important for you and put these into your programme first.
⊕ Fit other activities around these core essentials.
⊕ Arrange at least one training-and-preparation session for your team before the club. Go to the **GUARDIANS OF ANCORA** multimedia downloads area for training modules and tips, from basic to more involved topics.
⊕ Choose activities to bring out the best in your team: bear in mind their skills and experience.
⊕ Select the activities according to the children you are likely to have at the club: they should be the most important consideration when choosing the daily activities.
⊕ Children respond differently to the same activity. (Elder Guardians in particular should bear this in mind when planning activities for their Companies.)
⊕ If you have a long club, then you will be able to do more! The timings given are merely guidelines; different children will take different lengths of time to complete the same activity.
⊕ Be flexible in your timings, judge whether it would be more valuable to complete an activity, even though it may be overrunning, rather than cut it short and go on to the next activity.
⊕ Have something in your programme you can drop if things overrun.

SMALL GROUP TIME UNLOCK THE TREASURE

Part of *Unlock the treasure* is likely to be spent in construction and games: suitable activities are in the Treasure Store. There are two popular ways to run these: chat with your team about what will work well for your club.

- Every Company does the same game or activity on the same day. This requires a lot of resources and may limit the type of activity you use. It is easy to theme the activity closely with the Bible learning.
- Certain activities are set up every day and the Companies rotate around them. This needs fewer resources and an extra leader can run the activity, while the Elder Guardians have more time to interact with their Company; but your venue may not be large enough.

PROGRAMME ELEMENTS IN SUMMARY

Programme elements are listed in the table on page 23: the daily Quests, starting on page 35, give you activity material for each of these elements, every day of the club. Tick the ones you plan to use in your club – and remember, you can rearrange them in your own order. (We've put in a few ticks to start you off.)

For a two-hour club session, a popular timetable has a few minutes in small groups while everyone arrives; followed by a 45-minute 'all together' time; children then do activities in small groups for another 45 minutes; then come back together for a 20-minute 'all together' finish.

PROGRAMME ELEMENTS IN DETAIL

I ELDER GUARDIANS GATHER TEAM PREPARATION

Before the children arrive, have a short and focused team meeting. Each daily Quest gives suggestions for a brief reflection on the Bible story of the day and prompts for prayer. It also provides practical reminders to make sure everything is as ready as it can be before the children arrive.

II SIGN UP REGISTRATION

The first moments at **GUARDIANS OF ANCORA** are so important! Be welcoming, but not overwhelming, to assure parents that their children will be safe with you while also giving children a sense of the fun that they'll be having.

- Have enough people at the registration desk (especially on the first day) to show children and their parents to the right groups.

- Make sure that the registration desk is well organised, with spare forms and pens for any parents who want to register their children at the door.
- Have a floor plan of your venue to show where each team is sited, so that parents can find their way round.
- Ideally, display a large plan nearby so that parents bringing several children can check, without clogging up the registration area.
- Ensure parents have filled in a collection slip so you know who will be picking the child up at the end of the session. Collection slips and registration forms are available at the **GUARDIANS OF ANCORA** multimedia downloads area.
- Before the children go into the club, check they are wearing a name badge and give them each a paper firebug.

III COMPANY DUTIES SETTLING IN AND BUILDING RELATIONSHIPS

While children are arriving, this is an important time for relationship building in individual Company groups.

- As the week goes on, Company duties can include practising the *Learn and remember* verse, chatting about the Bible story from previous days and sharing news.
- Any child with jokes, pictures, messages or questions should place them in the Treasure Chest as they arrive.

IV GUARDIANS ASSEMBLE! ALL TOGETHER FOR OPENING SESSION

Bring everyone together for a fast-moving and fun opening session. This is led from the front and contains the main biblical teaching for the day's quest.

ANCORA HERALD NEWS OF THE CITY

The Shiner knows all about Ancora: each day, he brings the latest news reports. Being the Shiner, though, his tales may appear rather unbelievable!

TREASURE HUNT WHOLE-CLUB CHALLENGE TO FIND TODAY'S MISSING STORY-TREASURE

Each day, there is a challenge to find a missing story-treasure and bring it back to the Hall of Memory. At least one leader and a small number of children take the challenge, with everyone else cheering them on.

GUARDIANS SING GUARDIANS OF ANCORA THEME SONG – AND MORE!

It's great to have a number of musicians playing a variety of instruments, but if this is not feasible, use backing tracks, or simply sing along to a CD/MP3:

- Choose and practise the songs beforehand.
- Mix new songs and a few old favourites, including songs about God and faith, so that children are not singing words they might not believe.
- Sing the **GUARDIANS OF ANCORA** theme song every day, in the opening session and finale.

PROGRAMME ELEMENTS

TITLE	WHAT IT IS	TIME (APPROX)	CHILDREN	TEAM	TICK
Elder Guardians gather	Team preparation	30 minutes		Whole team	✓
Sign up	Registration		Individually	Registration team	✓
Company duties	Settling in; building relationships	10 minutes	Small groups	Elder Guardians and Apprentices	
Guardians assemble	Welcome	45 minutes	Everyone together	Keeper and Kal	✓
Ancora Herald	Setting the scene			The Shiner	
Treasure hunt	Challenge to find a missing artefact			Keeper and Kal	
Guardians sing	Theme song and more			Firebug band	
Story of the Saga	Bible storytelling			Fabula	✓
Guardians' guidelines	*Learn and remember* verse			Keeper, Kal, the Shiner	
Guardians' gold	Interview a team member			Keeper and Kal	
Unlock the treasure	Group time	45 minutes	Small groups	Elder Guardians	
Victuals	Refreshments			Refreshment team	✓
Treasure map	Bible discovery			Elder Guardians	✓
Orison	Prayer			Elder Guardians	✓
Construction	Construction/craft			Elder Guardians	
Games	Games			Elder Guardians	
Guardians' gathering		20 minutes	Everyone together	Keeper and Kal	
Treasure chest	Postbox			Kal or the Shiner	
Company showcase	'show and tell' for one company			Keeper, Kal, Elder Guardians	
The Search for the Golden Shield	Drama			Drama team/Swift	
Keeper's questions	Facts-based quiz			Keeper	
Benison	Praying together			Keeper, Kal	
Revive!	Finale (with theme song)			Everyone, with Firebug band	✓
Signing off	Waiting to go	10 minutes	Small groups	Elder Guardians	
Restoration	Clear up; debrief	30 minutes		Whole team	✓

STORY OF THE SAGA BIBLE STORYTELLING

This is the main storytelling section of the club, with a choice of ways of telling the day's Bible story, each day.

The **GUARDIANS OF ANCORA** multimedia download area gives access to five video storytelling episodes, helping you tell the Bible story. If you don't have any strong storytellers, you may choose the videos as the primary storytelling tool. Alternatively, you might choose to do the live retelling and reinforce it with the video.

GUARDIANS' GUIDELINES *LEARN AND REMEMBER* VERSE

'Jesus said: Love the Lord your God with all your heart, soul and mind.' Matthew 22:37 (CEV)

Each Quest will suggest a way of memorising this verse, with a song version too, and a few words to help children understand the meaning of the verse as well as being able to recite it.

Older children may like to learn verses 38 and 39 as well.

GUARDIANS' GOLD INTERVIEW A TEAM MEMBER

Children learn a lot from hearing the story of other people's lives, and all team members are role models for the children. Hearing a small part of a team member's journey of faith is very valuable. Each Quest suggests a topic for the interview.

V **UNLOCK THE TREASURE** TIME SPENT IN COMPANIES

The children move to their Companies for Bible exploration, construction, games and refreshments. Encourage team members to see this time as an opportunity to build positive relationships with the children.

VICTUALS REFRESHMENTS

Make sure you have refreshments that are suitable for children of other faiths. The easiest way to do this is to provide food suitable for vegetarians (no gelatine) and which contains no pork products. Do tell everyone that the food is OK otherwise they might assume it isn't and not have any.

TREASURE MAP BIBLE DISCOVERY

The Elder Guardians help the children explore the story in the Bible. Our aim is to help them to learn how to read the Bible for themselves and think about how it relates to their lives, as they read the story they have just heard. The *Guardian's Journal* (8–11s) or the *Guardian's Stories* (5–8s) will guide the children as they engage with the Bible.

Each day in *Bible discovery* help children find the story in the Bible or in their Guardian's booklets and learn to look for answers there. Use a translation that is easy for children to read (Good News Bible, Contemporary English Version, New Century Version or International Children's Bible).

It is important that Elder Guardians have prepared for this key part of the programme, where children have explicit opportunities to respond to God. The leaders' notes for each Quest are also available to download from the **GUARDIANS OF ANCORA** multimedia downloads area.

ORISON PRAYING IN SMALL GROUPS
Literally, a 'prayer': in each Quest there is a suggestion for how the Guardians might talk with God. This is connected with the material in *Guardian's Journal* or *Guardian's Stories*. Encourage every child to join in, whether silently or out loud.

CONSTRUCTION CRAFT
There are two types of construction: story-based constructions that link with each Quest's Bible teaching and Ancora-based constructions that follow the theme of the club and can be done on any day.

Whichever projects you choose to do, the construction time creates an environment where you can strengthen relationships, chat about the day's teaching and have fun together. The construction projects can be found in the Treasure Store on pages 80 to 83, or for further inspiration, see *Ultimate Craft*.

GAMES
The games time is another good opportunity for leaders and children to chat, build relationships and to demonstrate biblical values in the way the games are played. Make sure you risk-assess these activities and collect all the necessary materials beforehand.

Games used during **GUARDIANS OF ANCORA** can be found on pages 84 to 86. For further inspiration, see *Ultimate Games*, which contains hundreds of ideas that might be suitable for your club.

VI GUARDIANS' GATHERING
ALL TOGETHER AGAIN FOR THE CLOSING SESSION

During this time, the children are all together for another session of activities, led from the front.

TREASURE CHEST POSTBOX
Decorate a box as your Treasure Chest and set it up prominently near the stage. Kal or the Shiner can explain on the first day that this is where children can post their jokes, pictures, messages and questions. Start your Guardians' gathering each day by reading out and showing a selection of these.

COMPANY SHOWCASE 'SHOW AND TELL' FOR ONE COMPANY
Invite members of one company to show everyone something they have been doing, perhaps a Company emblem they have designed or a motto to shout. Interview a confident member of the Company, asking them what they're enjoying about Guardians of Ancora and what they have discovered today that they did not know before.

THE SEARCH FOR THE GOLDEN SHIELD DRAMA
The valiant Guardian Swift has faced many puzzling and dangerous quests in her search for missing artefacts for the Hall of Memory. As the daily drama unfolds, you will discover how and why she has earned her reputation as the bravest **GUARDIAN IN ANCORA**, and also what true treasure means to her.

KEEPER'S QUESTIONS FACTS-BASED QUIZ
This is a short quiz to recap the facts of the Bible story, test the children's memory of what they have been doing and hearing, and review the teaching points of the day. Questions for each Quest are available on pages 100 to 105 or to download, and you can add further questions of your own.

Vary the style of questions (ask for a straight answer; choice of two or three answers; visual clues). Decide whether you want to use the same method of scorekeeping or use a different one each day.

BENISON PRAYING TOGETHER
Literally, a 'blessing' or 'benediction': each Quest will give suggestions for encouraging your Guardians to talk with God, as they move towards a positive ending to the day.

REVIVE! FINALE, INCLUDING A REPRISE OF THE THEME SONG
Wrap up the all together time with the theme song and maybe another song the children have enjoyed. Tell children what might be happening the next day to whet their appetites and remind them about the procedure for being collected by parents and carers. Aim to finish on a high point.

VII SIGNING OFF BACK INTO COMPANIES WHILE WAITING TO BE COLLECTED

This is a winding-down time when you can:
⊕ use the activity suggestion in each Quest, while you wait for the Guardians to be collected
⊕ finish off anything from the day's Company duties
⊕ make sure the children have everything they need to take with them
⊕ say goodbye and encourage the children to come again next time
⊕ chat with those collecting their children.

VIII RESTORATION CLEARING UP AND A QUICK DEBRIEF

It may be that some of the team have their own children at **GUARDIANS OF ANCORA** and are unable to stay for long when the programme ends. Try to call everyone together to check any problems, briefly reminding them of tomorrow's activities and pray for the Holy Spirit to be at work in the children.

If you have time and the facilities, the team could share lunch together to round off the day.

THE BASICS V
NUTS AND BOLTS

WHO, WHERE AND WHEN

WHO WILL YOU INVITE TO GUARDIANS OF ANCORA?

Look at the list of aims you drew up (page 8). Do your aims relate to
⊕ the children already involved in your church
⊕ those outside it
⊕ both?

HOW MANY CHILDREN DO YOU WANT TO INVOLVE?

If your main aim is to get to know the children better, you might need to restrict numbers. On the other hand, if you want to present the gospel to children who haven't heard it, you may want as many as possible to attend. The number of leaders you have will affect your child capacity in order to meet the required adult:child ratio. You may also have limits imposed by the size of your venue.

WHAT AGE RANGE(S) DO YOU WANT TO TARGET WITH GUARDIANS OF ANCORA?

⊕ Do you want to cater for an age range that is already well-represented in your groups, or one that isn't?
⊕ Will you and your team be able to tailor the activities in a way that will appeal to a wide age range? Or will you target a narrower age range?
⊕ What training would help your team?

The **GUARDIANS OF ANCORA** holiday club is designed for use with children between the ages of 5 and 11. You can find parallel programmes for Under-5s and 11 to 14s in the **GUARDIANS OF ANCORA** multimedia downloads area.

WHERE AND WHEN?

If you run a holiday club regularly, you may already know when and where you will be meeting.

Any club needs to fix the date early enough for people to take it into account when they book their holidays: this affects potential leaders' availability and also children who want to attend. It is not unusual for families to plan their holidays around a church club date!

Think about potential clashes with:
⊕ other holiday clubs in the area
⊕ activities already booked at your premises
⊕ holidays and events organised by local schools
⊕ holidays or camps for local Boys' Brigade, Girls' Brigade, Cub or Brownie groups
⊕ carnivals or local events.

Or look at this another way and see if there is a way you can – intentionally – tie in your club with these events and benefit from the buzz around the local area.

Are other local churches running holiday clubs? Could you work together to maximise the impact in your area?
⊕ Run one big club?
⊕ Coordinate a sequence of clubs, on different dates with different programmes?
⊕ Share publicity?

TIME OF YEAR?

The summer break is the most obvious and popular time to hold your club. The potential leaders' availability will have the most effect on the duration of your holiday club. If most of your leaders need to take time off work, it may not be practical to run a full five-day club.

Consider also:
⊕ running the club in a half-term holiday or the Easter holidays
⊕ holding the club on Sundays through the holiday period, if your other sessions stop running
⊕ running the club on the same day of the week, through the holiday period.

LENGTH OF SESSION
⊕ Will you run your club just in the morning or just in the afternoon? For a longer day?
⊕ Will you include evening sessions for whole families or extra 'fun days' at the weekends?

PUBLICITY AND CLUB ADMIN

Ensure you have plenty of children at your holiday club through effective use of publicity and promotional materials. Plan this as carefully as other aspects of your club: it's easy to spend a lot of time and money without getting your message to those you want to hear and respond.
⊕ Remember the aims you have chosen for your club (page 8). Target your publicity to help you begin to meet those aims.
⊕ Make your publicity colourful and eye-catching: use the **GUARDIANS OF ANCORA** logo (available from the **GUARDIANS OF ANCORA** multimedia downloads area), an attractive, child-friendly font, pictures and clip art.
⊕ The publicity team can also organise themed administration paperwork for the club.

PUBLICITY IN SUMMARY

TYPE OF PUBLICITY	WHEN	USEFUL FOR YOUR CLUB?
Posters/fliers	Before	
Direct letters or invitation cards, application forms, follow-up letters	Before	
School assemblies	Before	
Press releases	Before, during, after	
Church services and notices	Before	
Special church services	Before, after	
Social media	Before, during, after	
Prayer cards or alerts	Before, during, after	

EXTERNAL PUBLICITY IN DETAIL

POSTERS/FLIERS
Use these to publicise **GUARDIANS OF ANCORA** in your local area. Good for raising awareness generally but not so effective at reaching your target audience.

DIRECT LETTERS OR INVITATION CARDS
Send or take a letter or invitation card to every child or family your church has contact with. Or distribute letters to all the children in your area, maybe through the local schools. (Make sure you do this well before the end of term, if you are having the club in a school holiday

period.) The benefit of direct communication is that you will know this has reached your audience. If you enclose an application/registration form to be returned to you, your admin will be easier, on the first day of your club.

You could also have a follow-up letter with more information, a consent/medical form, and perhaps a **GUARDIANS OF ANCORA** badge.

SCHOOL ASSEMBLIES

You may have a local Christian schools worker, or people from your church who are involved in schools ministry, or there may be church members who are teachers in the locality. If so, they could promote **GUARDIANS OF ANCORA** in a school assembly, if the school is happy for them to do so.

⊕ Do be clear about the capacity of your club, if numbers need to be restricted.

⊕ Make sure your team are prepared to meet children who may not be used to a faith environment.

⊕ If possible, involve the person who ran the assembly on the holiday club team so non-church children will have someone they recognise.

There are ideas for an assembly in the **GUARDIANS OF ANCORA** multimedia downloads area.

PRESS RELEASES

Holiday clubs provide the kind of story that local radio and papers love to cover in holiday periods when news is scanty. This can increase the appeal of your holiday club and show that the church(es) involved are reaching out into your local community. A press story may run during or after your holiday club so may not help bring children to the club.

Paid-for press advertisements are expensive but may be worth considering if you are working with other churches, across your locality.

There's a sample press release at the **GUARDIANS OF ANCORA** multimedia downloads area.

CHURCH SERVICES AND NOTICES

It's easy to forget to tell the people you know! Publicise the holiday club at your own church and other churches in your local area.

SPECIAL CHURCH SERVICES

On the Sunday before the first service of the club, include a section of the regular church service where the team will be formally commissioned. Recognition by the whole church family will give a practical and spiritual boost to the team.

SOCIAL MEDIA

Make use of any social media routes used by members of your church.

Consider setting up an invitation-only group or email list for your team, to circulate news, information and encouragement. For many people, this is a primary communication tool so make good use of it for your club.

Be aware of your church safeguarding policy and data protection issues (see page 30).

PRAYER CARDS OR ALERTS

It is important to keep your church informed about the club. Prayer cards, bookmarks or emails can help church members pray before, during and after **GUARDIANS OF ANCORA**. Again, be aware of your church safeguarding policy and data protection issues (see page 30).

PUBLICITY MATERIAL

Turn to the inside back cover to find publicity materials available from Christian Publicity Organisation.

Visit the **GUARDIANS OF ANCORA** multimedia downloads area for logos and posters to print yourself.

Please mention Scripture Union in your promotional activity since positive publicity ultimately allows SU to develop more resources like this holiday club material.

HOLIDAY CLUB ADMIN

These should use the same typeface and colours as other materials to maintain the consistent **GUARDIANS OF ANCORA** scheme.

⊕ Remember to budget for paper, printing and photocopying costs (it can mount up quickly).

⊕ Get as much of this as possible done well before the club: printers have a nasty habit of going wrong at the last minute!

BEFORE GUARDIANS OF ANCORA		
Item	Purpose	Quantity
Volunteer forms	For potential team members, including an indication of roles they'd like to take on	
Safeguarding forms	For team members who do not already have clearance	
Notes and training materials for the team	Even if someone else writes this material, the printing and publicity team should be responsible for the layout	

DURING GUARDIANS OF ANCORA		
Item	Purpose	Quantity
Registration forms	For children to complete	
Consent forms	For parents/carers/Elders	
Collection slips	For parents/carers/Elders	
Name badges	For the team members and for any adults who are on site and part of **GUARDIANS OF ANCORA**	
Signs and notices	These will be needed around the site, including the main meeting area, entrances, toilets, exits and areas that are out of bounds	

Visit the **GUARDIANS OF ANCORA** multimedia downloads area to print registration forms, consent forms and collection slips.

FINANCES

Consider your financial resources. Work out what you need money for. Do you have a budget from your church? Will you need to do some fundraising? Will you charge for children to attend **GUARDIANS OF ANCORA**?

THINK ABOUT >>>

The first child in a family could be charged, with a reduction for subsequent children.

Research shows that, in many cases, making a charge for a club has no effect on the number of children who come.

Parents often value a club they have had to pay for more highly than something that is free.

Item	Budget
Hire of premises	
Hire of equipment	
GUARDIANS OF ANCORA resource books	
Guardian's Journals and *Guardian's Stories*	
Publicity	
Craft materials	
Refreshments	
Scenery	
Printing and photocopying	
Prizes or presents for the children	

LEGAL REQUIREMENTS

There are various legal requirements you will need to be familiar with and conform to as you prepare for your holiday club. These include having a safeguarding or child protection policy in place, providing adequate space in your venue, meeting adult to child ratios, registering your club and insurance. To obtain up-to-date information on all of these requirements, go to 'Legal requirements for running a club' on the **GUARDIANS OF ANCORA** multimedia downloads area.

Remind all your team about these legal requirements – even those who are familiar with the venue and with working with children. Include it in your planning, briefings and any training you run.

SAFEGUARDING

All churches should already have a clear safeguarding and child protection policy. Ensure that your holiday club team are familiar with it and it is carried out. Most churches have a designated person to be the safeguarding officer. Your holiday club team need to know they should talk to this person first if they have any concerns about the safety or welfare of a child. For more information, go to the **GUARDIANS OF ANCORA** multimedia downloads area or the Churches' Child Protection Advisory Service www.ccpas.co.uk.

Talk with your church's safeguarding officer to make sure members of your team have the necessary paperwork, in good time for the club.

DATA PROTECTION

How will you maintain the confidentiality of the information you receive on the registration forms? Make sure you abide by the principles of the Data Protection Act. Visit dataprotectionact.org for more information, including the eight principles of protecting data.

ACCIDENTS AND FIRST AID

Aim for there to be at least one person appointed as a first-aider (see Basics 3) with a current first-aid certificate and access to an up-to-date first-aid kit. (This is not a legal requirement but it is important to take reasonable precautions to oversee the welfare of those in your care.) The whole team should know who is responsible for first aid. You will need an accident book to record any incidents, which is essential in the event of an insurance claim. The matter should be recorded, however small, along with details of the action taken. For other health and safety information visit www.rospa.com.

RISK ASSESSMENT AND FIRE PROCEDURES

The health and safety person on your team needs to make sure all the activities are adequately risk assessed before the club starts, and plan how you will evacuate the building in the event of a fire. This person is in charge of clearing the building and dealing with the emergency services, but they should allocate responsibility for checking other areas of the building (toilets, snack bar and so on) to other team members who will be present each day.

Invent catchy slogans to remind the children where the toilets are and what to do, if the fire alarm sounds. One holiday club teaches: 'If there is a fire don't scream and shout, go through those doors and you'll soon get out.'

It is essential the whole team knows emergency procedures, including fire exits and assembly points, and where to access a telephone in case of emergency.

- ⊕ You may want to incorporate a fire drill into your programme early in the week. (The children will be used to this from school, but it might help the adults!)
- ⊕ Check that fire escapes are kept clear.
- ⊕ Make sure the team know the position of fire extinguishers and know what the fire alarm – or noise that means 'leave the building immediately' – sounds like.
- ⊕ Each Elder Guardian should be a roll-call marshal for their Company.

FOOD HYGIENE

Refer to your church's health and safety policy if you are going to be cooking or handling food during the club.

CHILDREN WITH ADDITIONAL NEEDS

It is quite possible you will have children with any combination of additional needs attending your holiday club. There are a few things you can do in advance that would help these children to settle more quickly.

- ⊕ Make sure you have as much useful information about the children as possible before the holiday club starts. Find out from parents or carers what would help their child the most.
- ⊕ Invite children who struggle with change to arrive early so they can look around, meet leaders and settle in before all the other children arrive.
- ⊕ It's also helpful to give a basic outline, in order, of the daily activities to the parents or carers of these children, and ask if they can help you produce a visual timetable for their child.
- ⊕ Make sure you have alternative formats of words and visuals you show on screens for children who won't be able to see or read them. Find out the best format for the children who may need them.
- ⊕ Make sure the way your rooms are set out allows easy wheelchair access without having to move lots of chairs or tables out of the way.
- ⊕ Have leaders available who can buddy children who need one-to-one care.
- ⊕ Try to allocate a quiet room for children who need 'space' from time to time.

THE BASICS VI

TIMETABLE AND PLANNER

Here is a sample timetable/planner for organising your holiday club.

This is an ideal, so don't feel put off if you haven't been able to start your planning as early as suggested. Work out how much time you actually have, then distribute the tasks below within it.

And remember that the overall club co-coordinator will have a lot of checking to do – but it does not all have to be done by you!

GUARDIANS OF ANCORA HOLIDAY CLUB TIMETABLE AND PLANNER PART 1		
DATE	**ACTION**	**NOTES**
One year ahead	If you have just finished a club, make sure you have contact details for team and children; let them know you expect to hold holiday club again.	
8 months before	'Pencil in' names for your core planning team.	
	Agree dates. Make provisional venue booking.	
	Confirm 'holiday club services' dates with church leader.	
	Request budget or launch fundraising.	
6 months before	Book assembly slot at local school(s).	
5 months before	Confirm members of core team; book first planning session.	
	Go into 'active organising' mode at church; launch prayer support.	
4 months before	**FIRST CORE TEAM MEETING** (Decide theme; review or choose resources.)	
	Order resources.	
	Download further resources from the **GUARDIANS OF ANCORA** multimedia downloads area.	
	Hand out resource books to core team to read, reflect and pray.	
	Confirm venue booking.	

GUARDIANS OF ANCORA HOLIDAY CLUB TIMETABLE AND PLANNER PART 2

DATE	ACTION	NOTES
	Appoint publicity and printing person/team.	
	Liaise with church safeguarding officer to verify team paperwork.	
	Book anyone with specialist skills.	
3 months before	**SECOND CORE TEAM MEETING** (Agree daily timetable; watch story downloads and listen to theme song; confirm team roles.)	
	Appoint upfront presenters; technical manager; drama leader	
	Book 'whole team' planning meeting; invite all.	
	Check what equipment and resources are available.	
	Work out your 'shopping list' of specific items: see what people will donate, before buying.	
10 weeks before	Have registration paperwork printed; or set up online registration.	
9 weeks before	Arrange provision for very young children of team members.	
8 weeks before	**THIRD CORE TEAM MEETING** (Further daily planning; plan extra events; consider contingencies [rainy weather etc].)	
	Confirm team members with specific roles and duties, ahead of 'all team' planning meeting.	
7 weeks before	Record and confirm applications and consent forms as they come in.	
6 weeks before	Assembly with local school(s), with application forms.	
	Brief worship leaders for holiday club services.	
	Make sure any unusual items or equipment are arranged.	
5 weeks before	Final preparation for all-team meeting; prepare paperwork; plan agenda.	
	Start allocating children to groups.	
4 weeks before	**ALL-TEAM MEETING** (Run through everything; team training on **GUARDIANS OF ANCORA**; give theme song to band; agree set-up day; pray together.)	
	Communicate team lists and roles to whole team; make sure team have their briefing information.	
	Prepare checklist for 'set up' and 'clear away'.	
3 weeks before	Keep in touch with key team members and help problem solve.	
	Confirm details with service leader.	

GUARDIANS OF ANCORA **HOLIDAY CLUB TIMETABLE AND PLANNER** PART 3

DATE	ACTION	NOTES
2 weeks before	Monitor progress in all areas.	
Sunday before	Commissioning for whole team during regular church service.	
1 week before	Final shopping.	
	Check signs, notes and lists are ready.	
Day before	Set up the venue as much as possible.	
1st service	Contribute to the service.	
Days of the club	Arrive early!	
	Attend team meeting before the club; give the day's briefing to all.	
	Monitor registration/children arriving.	
	Be available during the club session as the 'go to' person for any problems arising.	
	Keep track of time.	
	Monitor children leaving.	
	Help clear up.	
	Short debrief on any key matters arising.	
	Thank and enthuse the team for tomorrow.	
	Make sure all is safe, clean and locked up for the next club session.	
Bonus event(s)	(eg) Games, fun, barbecue for club families-and-friends, end of club party.	
2nd service	Contribute to the service.	
Afterwards	Help with final clear-up of the venue.	
	Sort out outstanding admin: balance budget.	
	Check follow-up press release has gone out.	
	Thank all the team personally.	
	Make sure you have contact details for team and children so you can invite them to other events, club reunions, special services and your next holiday club.	
	Informal review meeting for full team, perhaps with a meal, to evaluate the club.	
	… and relax!	

Thanks to all the holiday club coordinators who helped compile this timetable, especially Jenny, Simon, Shera and Margaret.

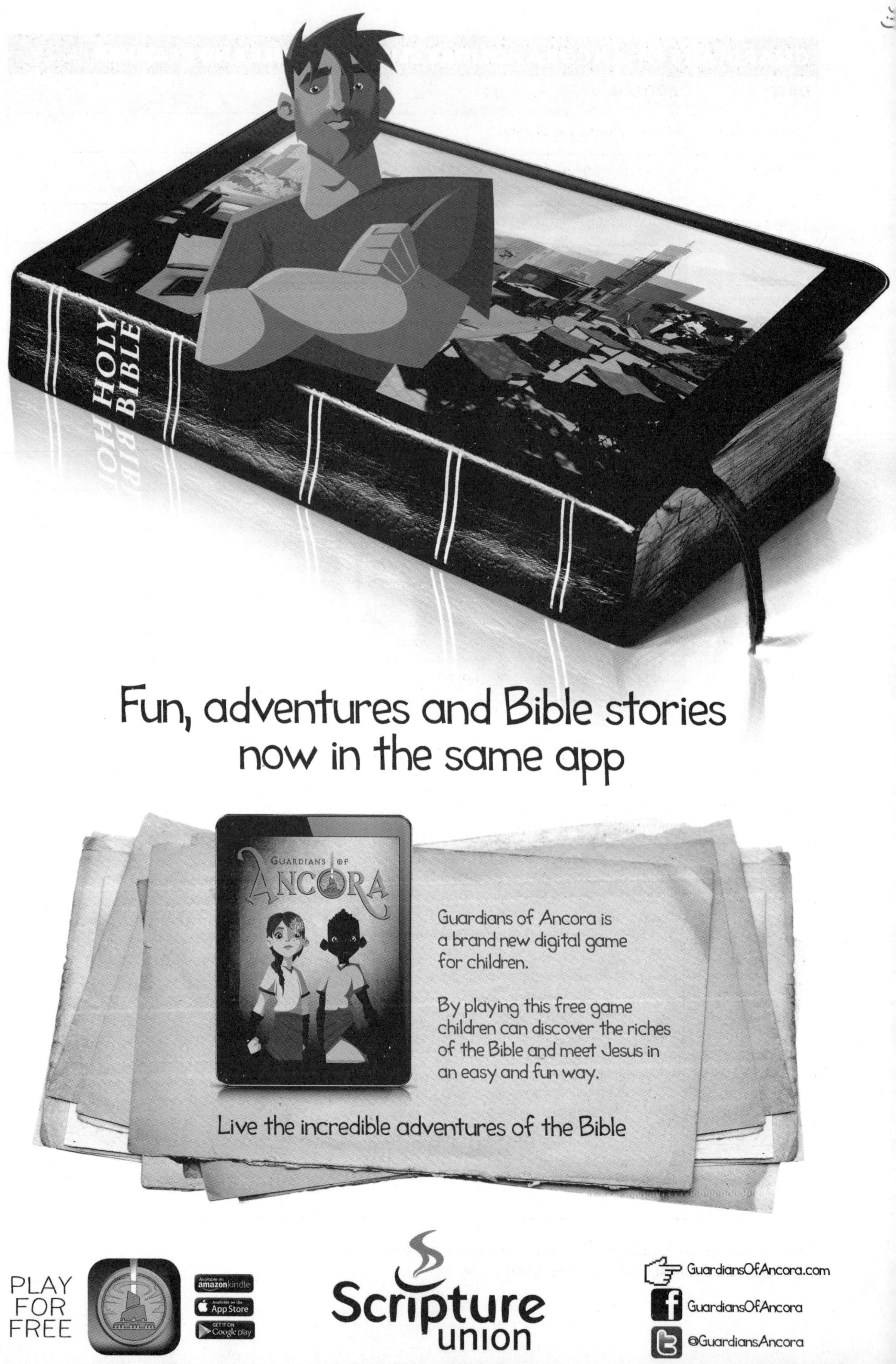

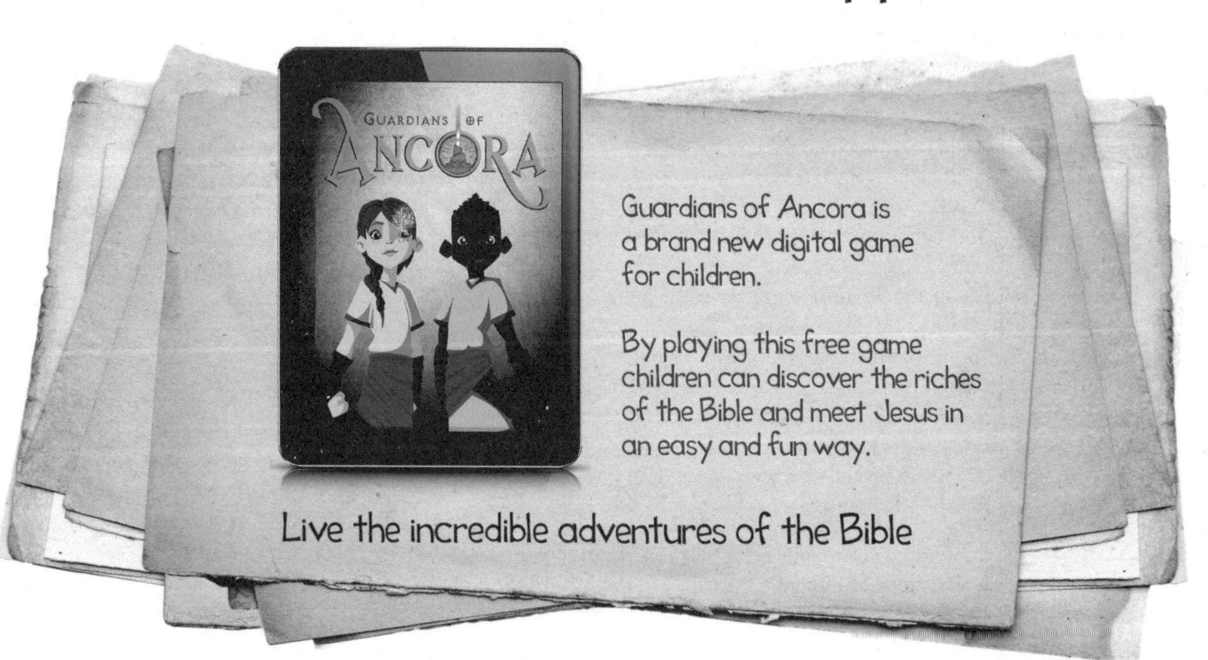

Fun, adventures and Bible stories now in the same app

Live the incredible adventures of the Bible

THE QUESTS

TREASURE SEEKING DAY BY DAY

SERVICE 1
WHO IS JESUS?

BACKGROUND
(CHILDREN AND THEIR FAMILIES)

NO CHURCH BACKGROUND
Children and adults will be present in church for a variety of reasons. Adults may have come to accompany the children but have little interest in the Christian faith. On the other hand, they themselves may be searching for God and registering their child for **GUARDIANS OF ANCORA** may be part of their faith journey. The children will also have mixed experiences of church and understanding of the Christian faith. Each of them needs to be welcomed and helped to enjoy the service. Think about what will be unfamiliar to them, for example when to stand and when to sit, and what words they may not understand. It's good to involve familiar faces in the service if possible, such as a schools worker who has led assemblies at the local school or the leader of the community toddlers' group.

CHURCH CHILDREN
Encourage church children to look out for their friends who don't usually come and sit with them to help them feel part of what is going on. Some church children could take part in the service. By involving them you can help them feel part of the holiday club in a special way.

FROM OTHER FAITHS
If you do have children and their families coming to this first service, make sure they receive a genuine but not overwhelming welcome. It may be their first visit to a church, so have someone on hand to explain what is happening throughout the service and to reassure them that it's OK just to watch and listen rather than join in the singing or prayers. At the end, introduce them to other children and families with whom they could form friendships. If they are coming to a church service they will expect it to be a Christian act of worship, so there is no need to 'water down' the message.

WITH ADDITIONAL NEEDS
Parents will value your non-judgemental acceptance of their child. Ask parents or carers how best to welcome their child, since they need to be confident that their child will be included, encouraged and kept safe. As you begin to make friends with the child, assume that they are able to understand you. Just because a child cannot speak, move or see does not mean that they do not understand. Each child will want to be treated the same as any other child of the same age.

SERVICE PREPARATION

WHAT-YOU-NEED CHECKLIST:

- ☐ Paper and pencils

- ☐ Twelve name-of-month labels (available from the **GUARDIANS OF ANCORA** multimedia downloads area)

- ☐ Drama script from page 88

- ☐ The following on large strips of card in the shape of luggage labels, with space to tick them or cross them out: John the Baptist?, Elijah?, Jeremiah?, a prophet?, the Messiah?, the Son of the living God?

- ☐ A small bag or piece of luggage to attach each label to. The bags and their labels should be hidden (in fairly plain sight!) prior to the start of the service.

- ☐ A marker pen

- ☐ Four long labels on which are written: Jesus who heals (vertically); Jesus who cares (vertically); Jesus the friend (horizontally); Jesus is alive! (horizontally).

SUGGESTED SONGS

- ⊕ 'Who was the man?' *Light for Everyone* CD
- ⊕ 'The virgin Mary had a baby boy' *Junior Praise* 251
- ⊕ 'Who took fish and bread?' *Junior Praise* 286
- ⊕ 'Come on and celebrate!' *Mission Praise* 99
- ⊕ 'You are the King of glory' *Mission Praise* 790
- ⊕ 'With a prayer you fed the hungry'
- ⊕ **GUARDIANS OF ANCORA** theme song
- ⊕ *Learn and remember* verse song

THE SERVICE

WELCOME

It is particularly important in this service that the service leader introduces him or herself – important because there may be visitors and this is an introduction to the holiday club, but also important because the theme of this service is identifying who people are, especially who Jesus is. But first welcome everyone in the name of Jesus Christ and explain that you gather together regularly to worship God the Father, God the Son and God the Holy Spirit.

SET THE SCENE

Explain who you are (giving your full name and possibly a nickname), your role in **GUARDIANS OF ANCORA**, your roles in your family, at work, in the community, in the church and something about your past. Use PowerPoint images and photos, if possible. Conclude by saying, 'And now you know who I am… or do you?'

Say that in the service you are going to explore how we know people and what we know about them and, especially, what we know about who Jesus is. The children will be finding out much more about Jesus during the holiday club.

INTRODUCTORY ACTIVITY

Invite everyone to join in the quest of discovering the people who share the same birth month as they do. Challenge them to write down their names or, even better, stick together becoming a larger and larger group. Say they have just four minutes to do this. Younger children will need to be accompanied by an adult who will not be joining in the quest for themselves (unless they share the same birth month as their child!).

Alternatively, designate twelve areas of the room or worship area for the twelve months of the year, and invite people to gather by the appropriate one – although this makes it less of a quest or challenge.

Ask what people have discovered about others. What can they say about them?

THE SEARCH FOR THE GOLDEN SHIELD

Introduce the club drama: *The Search for the Golden Shield*. Explain that, throughout the club, you'll be catching up with the adventures of Swift and Dash, newly graduated Guardians. Today, they look forward to their lives looking for story-treasures.

BIBLE READING

As you begin, ask for a volunteer to come to the front and be a Guardian. Their task will be to find some hidden objects and help you to find out how they contribute to today's story.

Explain to the Guardian that there are several 'clues' around the room, each belonging to different people. Ask the Guardian to search for these items and bring them to you. Encourage the congregation to help if they can see a 'clue' near their seats. After all bags and labels have been brought to you, say that lots of people seem to have left their luggage behind, while noticing that some of their names seem rather odd. Conclude that they must have something to do with today's story, and perhaps they will help us to discover something we didn't know before. Ask your volunteer to return to their seat.

Explain that, throughout his life, Jesus gave lots of clues about who he was, but people didn't always pick up on the clues or simply did not understand them. 'The Son of Man' was Jesus' favourite way of speaking about himself. Although it sounds a bit odd to us today, it didn't seem odd to those who knew him. They would have connected it with the heavenly figure mentioned in Daniel 7, and since then Christians have seen this as indirect evidence of Jesus' heavenly divinity.

The conversation that Jesus has in Matthew 16 is with his disciples and happens at the start of his journey towards Jerusalem. He knows he is going there to die (v 21). He's preparing his disciples.

Matthew 16:13–16,21 lends itself to a dramatic reading, with a narrator, Jesus, the disciples and Simon Peter. After each comment on Jesus' identity, there should be a pause as each title or name is held up using the luggage labels from earlier: John the Baptist?; Elijah?; Jeremiah?; a prophet?; the Messiah?; the Son of the living God?

(These titles and names could also be displayed as a PowerPoint.)

The narrator should step forward, away from the other readers, to read verse 21, with a voice that communicates to the listeners that this is an explanatory clue about Jesus' identity and his role.

BIBLE TALK

The Bible talk explores who and what Jesus is, and who he is not! Jesus had a name and a job title (Jesus, the Christ/Messiah, the One chosen by God, Son of the living God), but his identity was far more than that. It was only after his death, his resurrection and the coming of the Holy Spirit that this would become clearer.

Jesus' disciples have been with him for around three years. They have come to understand that he is the Messiah (although they don't know exactly what that means). They have got to know and love him. Note that, when Simon Peter blurts out that Jesus is the Son of the living God, he is not necessarily recognising Jesus' divinity so much as another way of saying Jesus is the Messiah!

WHO WAS JESUS? WHAT'S IN A NAME?

Ask:

- ⊕ Who has just found out the name of someone who shares their birth month?
- ⊕ Why do we have a name?
- ⊕ Who shares a name with someone in their class/family/place of work? How do people know the difference between you? (surname, nickname, descriptive label, eg goalie Harry, tall Maddie)

STORY

Jesus often calls himself the Son of Man, which suggests to people who knew him that he had come from heaven. The people in our Bible reading today were puzzled by who Jesus really was. Some said that Jesus was someone from the past who had come back to life. Who can remember the names of the men they thought he was?

Show again the three name labels from the Bible reading.

Show the John the Baptist label.

What can anyone tell me about John the Baptist? Is 'Baptist/Baptiser' his real name? (It was given to him because he preached and baptised people, preparing them for the coming of the Messiah.)

'John' is the name the angel told his father, Zechariah, to give to him (Luke 1:11–17). As a child he may well have been called 'John, son of Zechariah' to distinguish him from other boys called John.

Jesus is not John the Baptist, although they were cousins. (Jesus was known as 'the son of Joseph the carpenter' (Matthew 13:55).) By this time of this conversation, John has been put to death by King Herod (Matthew 14).

Cross out the label.

(Old joke: What do John the Baptist and Winnie the Pooh have in common? They share the same middle name.)

Show the Elijah label.

What can anyone tell me about Elijah? We read about him in 1 Kings 17 – 2 Kings 2. He was a brave prophet in the Old Testament who urged God's people, especially the kings of Israel, to turn back to God. People did not like Elijah and rejected what he said. John the Baptist is likened to Elijah (Luke 1:17). Jesus is not Elijah, although he meets with him on the mountain along with Moses soon after this conversation (Matthew 17:1–13). Elijah had gone to heaven centuries before. Like John the Baptist and Elijah, Jesus' enemies reject him and all that he says and stands for.

Cross out the label.

Show the Jeremiah label.

Who can tell me anything about Jeremiah? He was another brave messenger from God who urged God's people living in and around Jerusalem to be faithful to God. They did not listen and the people were taken away to live in another country, Babylon. Jesus was not Jeremiah.

Cross out the label.

Jesus' mother, Mary, and his adoptive father, Joseph, were both told what name to give Jesus long before he was born. He was to be called Jesus, which is the same as Joshua and means 'One who rescues or saves' (Matthew 1:21; Luke 1:31).

WHO WAS JESUS? WHAT'S IN A JOB TITLE?

Who knows the name of their teacher at school? Do you know their first name? What about your doctor? We often call a doctor or policeman by their title, not their name. We usually don't know a lot about their lives, apart from what they do for a job.

Show the prophet label.

Who knows what a prophet is? (It's someone sent from God who comes with a special message, usually about people's behaviour and occasionally about the future.) Jesus is far more than just a prophet, although he does tell people how to live in a way that pleases God and sometimes talked about the future.

Cross out the label.

Can anyone remember in our Bible reading what titles Simon Peter gave to Jesus?

Show the Messiah and Son of the living God labels.

We often call Jesus 'Christ', but that is a title not his name, like a job title. The word 'Christ' in ancient Greek means 'someone who is anointed or chosen'. The Hebrew word 'Messiah' means the same thing, as does the title 'Son of the living God'. The Jews were expecting someone to come to rescue them, someone who was specially chosen by God for the job.

Simon Peter has come to recognise that this is who Jesus is. After all he has spent so much time with Jesus. He has travelled with him and seen the wonderful things Jesus has said and done, the people he has healed and the poor and lonely people he has cared for. He has heard the spellbinding stories Jesus has told and the amazing things he has said about God. Jesus has come to rescue or save people, although Peter does not quite see how this works out in practice.

Tick the Messiah and Son of the living God labels.

WHO IS JESUS, REALLY?

Jesus is more than a name, more than an ordinary man, more than someone with a job. Simon Peter has only just begun to grasp this. It is only after Jesus has died and come alive again that Peter and the rest of Jesus' disciples can understand better. Listen again, as Jesus prepares his followers for the suffering and death he's going to have to face (read v 21).

Take the 'Messiah' and the 'Son of the living God' labels and form them into a cross shape.

During the holiday club the children will be sent on Quests and will find out far more about who Jesus is, what he came to do and what that means for us today.

PRAYER

During the prayers, place four labels, two vertically and two horizontally, to form a cross shape (either stuck on a board or held by three people). Members of the team or children could read these prayers.

Jesus Christ, you came to heal sick people. We pray for anyone we know who is ill or in pain. We ask you to be close to them and make them whole.

Jesus, Christ, hear our prayer.

Invite one person to hold 'Jesus who heals' high in the air.

Jesus Christ, you cared for people who were lonely or on the outside. We pray for those in our class or in our community or place of work for whom no one seems to care. Help us to show the love that you have for them.

Jesus, Christ, hear our prayer.

Invite the same person to add 'Jesus who cares' below, to form one long vertical piece.

Jesus Christ, you were a good friend to your followers. We thank you for our friends and ask that you will help us to be good friends in the way that you were.

Jesus, Christ, hear our prayer.

Ask a second person to hold 'Jesus the friend' out horizontally from the vertical piece, about two thirds of the way up.

Jesus Christ, you are alive today. We think of places in the world where there is war, suffering, hunger and fear [add specific contemporary examples]. We pray that in these places the power that made you alive again may change evil into good.

Jesus, Christ, hear our prayer. Amen

Invite the third person to hold 'Jesus is alive!' horizontally on the other side, forming the final piece of the cross.

If it is your tradition, join in saying The Lord's Prayer together.

QUEST 1
JESUS CALLS THE FISHERMEN

KEY PASSAGE
Luke 5:1–11

KEY STORYLINES

- The Guardians find a pile of fishing nets, which open up the story of the call of the fishermen.
- By listening to Jesus the fishermen are able to catch very large numbers of fish, when without him they had worked hard, but caught nothing.
- Jesus asks the fishermen to leave their homes and fish for people instead of fish. He calls them to follow him.

KEY AIMS
- To welcome each child to the club, setting the tone for the next few days.
- To find out that, just as Jesus called the fishermen to follow him, he calls us too.
- To understand that following Jesus is sometimes costly, but always brings blessing.
- To regard and treat these stories as wonderful treasure.

GUARDIANS BACKGROUND

NO CHURCH BACKGROUND
There are several things that you may need to explain for children with little or no church background:
- First, the phrase 'Word of God' – that Jesus was helping the crowd to understand their holy book (what Christians call the Old Testament).
- In those days it was common for religious teachers to wander around with their followers.
- Going out in the boat was a practical thing to stop the crowd from forcing him into the water!
- In verse 5, Simon was being sarcastic, because a fisherman would not need a carpenter/builder to teach him how to fish.
- That is why in verse 8 his reaction is so extreme. Although he doesn't know who Jesus is yet, he does know he is more than a teacher – so he does not think he is worthy to have Jesus stay on his boat, because he is far from perfect.
- Sin is not doing God's will.
- 'Fishing for men' is a metaphor for helping people to know God.

CHURCH CHILDREN
These children will know that Jesus is 'the Son of God' and may assume that anyone who heard Jesus teach would accept what he said straight away. They will have heard about Peter and may know other stories about him. So, this early encounter is helpful to show that everyone has to make a journey of faith as they grow to know Jesus better. The amazing catch of fish is interpreted by Peter as a blessing from God, reinforcing the authority of what Jesus is teaching. Peter and the other disciples are given the task of sharing God's good news to bring people to him – that is still true for followers of Jesus today.

WITH OTHER FAITHS
Muslims accept Jesus (Isa in Arabic) as a prophet. It would be easy to interpret the miracle of the catch of fish as God (Allah) showing that Jesus is a prophet. Although not conclusive, the fact that Peter calls Jesus 'Lord' and thinks that his own sinful nature (lack of perfection) means Jesus should not stay with him opens up the question of Jesus being more than a prophet. This is also blasphemy for Jewish children, for whom God is one. Emphasising Jesus' Jewish background, and that 'the Word of God' Jesus taught was their Scriptures may be helpful, as is getting them to think about what the Old Testament says about the coming Messiah. Hindu, Sikh and Jain children may know stories of gods coming to visit the earth. They need to know that Jesus was born and lived as a human being, while still being God.

WITH ADDITIONAL NEEDS
Some children with additional needs may take longer to settle in on the first day because everything is out of routine and strange. Because the programme is fast moving, give clear and repeated guidance. A visual diary with photos would help with this too. Fish will feature highly today, so why not have some tactile fish to hold during different parts of the programme, especially in the 'Bible Discovery' time. Choose one question from the 'With all Ages' section, and use a similar one every day. 'What have you learnt about Jesus from today's story?' would be a good one to use today.

ELDER **GUARDIANS** GATHER

SPIRITUAL PREPARATION

Read Luke 5:1–11 together.

Encourage the group to have a short time of reflection together, as you read the following:

Think about what it must have been like for the fishermen when they met Jesus. There was something about Jesus that the fishermen trusted; they'd only just met him, yet they dropped their nets and followed him. Ask yourself whether you would respond the same way, and what emotions you might feel as you obeyed. Jesus called the fishermen to follow him just as he calls us too. Think about the confidence that comes from knowing you are called.

Pause

Now think about the children who are coming – some with faith in God, others knowing nothing about him. Think about how your speech and actions will show whether they are welcome or not. What message will they receive about God if you do not make them feel accepted as they are?

After a few minutes, invite anyone who wants to to share their thoughts.

Finish with a time of prayer, praying for the children, even if you do not know who is coming; God does, so ask him to bless them and show himself to them by his Spirit and through the team.

PRACTICAL PREPARATION

Talk through the programme. Remind people of the key learning aims and who is doing what, making sure everyone knows their role and has everything they need. Check that younger team members or those who have not been involved before are OK. Encourage them during the session too. The overall leader could do this or it could be assigned to another member of the team, or member of the church whose sole role is to encourage the team. It is important that people feel able to ask about anything they are not 100 per cent clear about.

Make sure each Elder Guardian has a backpack, tools, firebugs and a lantern to share with their Company during the 'Treasure hunt'.

Set up the different areas of the club, making sure everything is in place in plenty of time, so you are ready as the first children come from the registration area. You will probably need extra help as it is the first day. Leaders should be especially welcoming to parents and children who have not been before or any adults accompanying children who look uncomfortable being in a church setting.

Listen to any last-minute information or instructions from the Guildmaster, Keeper or Kal, or from the drama, music or refreshment team. Remind the team to set an example of joining in and responding to prompts from the upfront presenters: this will encourage the children to get more involved.

As this is the first day of the club, make sure the registration team with extra helpers are ready to greet and register the children, so that any new children and parents don't have to wait long. Have a welcome team on hand to take the children to their Companies.

WHAT-YOU-NEED CHECKLIST

- [ ] **Registration:** registration forms, badges, labels, pens, team lists, paper firebugs
- [ ] **Company duties:** materials for your chosen opening and closing activities, including materials to make a name-plate
- [ ] **Ancora Herald:** today's news; small trifle; copies of the map of Ancora for each Company
- [ ] **Treasure hunt:** backpacks, tools, firebugs, fishing nets
- [ ] **Music:** Firebugs band or backing tracks
- [ ] **Story of the Saga:** fishing nets from 'Treasure hunt'; story script and visual aids; **GUARDIANS OF ANCORA** multimedia story downloads
- [ ] **Guardians' guidelines:** verse cards, time chart, timer
- [ ] **Victuals:** drinks and snacks
- [ ] **Treasure map:** Bibles, *Guardian's Journals* or *Guardian's Stories*, paper, pens, pencils
- [ ] **Orison:** fishing nets, ribbons
- [ ] **Construction:** materials for your chosen craft option(s)
- [ ] **Games:** equipment for your chosen game option(s)
- [ ] **Treasure Chest:** for jokes, messages, questions and pictures
- [ ] **Drama:** script from page 89, costumes and props
- [ ] **Keeper's questions:** quiz questions
- [ ] **Benison:** paper fish shapes and felt-tip pens

THE FIRST QUEST

COMPANY DUTIES
◷ 10 MINUTES

Leaders should be familiar with the names of expected children, and use the name of each child as much as they can. Introduce unknown children to one another.

Every Guardian will have a 'special Guardian skill'. Chat with the children to work out what this might be: discover something that each child is good at (not necessarily academic) and designate this as their skill – the more fun, the better. (For example: kind to animals; jumping; video gaming.)

On this first day of the club, invent a name for your small group: the Company of ——s. Involve the children in choosing the name, to give them an extra sense of belonging and ownership. Work together to make a large nameplate to put at the entrance to your Company space.

Reinforce this sense of belonging with a Company motto: something short, crisp and easy to remember. Decide on a motto and then use it as a password, each time the Company meets.

Design a company badge together and encourage the children to draw it on the title page of *Guardian's Stories* or *Guardian's Journal*.

In any time remaining, begin to decorate your Company space, making it unique to your group of children. Each child will have received a firebug at registration (they'll get a different coloured one each day). Use these as part of your decoration.

GUARDIANS ASSEMBLE
◷ 45 MINUTES ALL TOGETHER

Once all the children are settled, the Keeper of the Keys and Kal introduce themselves and then introduce Fabula and the Shiner (if you are featuring them). The upfront presenters set an enthusiastic and adventurous tone to the programme and welcome the children to the Hall of Memory in the city of Ancora.

The Keeper is idealistic. She tells the children that they are Guardians in the city of Ancora and emphasises what an honour it is to be part of the city Guild – and for the Guild to have such eager recruits. She explains why Ancora needs them so much: many of the story-treasures from the Hall of Memory have been lost – and with them, the stories of the Saga. Will the Guardians aid the city, in this time of need, find the missing treasures and restore them to the Hall? (YES!!)

Kal is practical. He establishes three ground rules for your club which might be:
⊕ what to do if the fire or smoke alarm goes off;
⊕ where the toilets are and whether you need to ask before you go;
⊕ your slogan or action to indicate 'stop' and that the children should pay attention.

Kal and the Keeper are about to tell the Guardians about today's Quest when they are interrupted by the Shiner. (If you are not using this character, have the 'news' arrive as a message for one of the presenters to read out.)

ANCORA HERALD
The Shiner announces his presence with some sort of sound: bells round his knees, castanets – the more peculiar, the better. Each day he brings news of the city, which he reads from a large sheet of paper. He is likely to have mislaid this, among his layers of clothing, gadgets and lanterns: he may need someone 'sensible', like Kal, to help him find it.

The Shiner performs this script:

> **Heed the headlines from the Herald,**
> **Whether you're called Bernice or Gerald!**
> **Listen or you'll get an eye full**
> **Of my lovely cabbage trifle!**

He produces a small trifle from his robes and gives it to the Keeper. As he reads the headlines, he shouts the words in capitals, as if he were a newspaper vendor on the street.

GUILDMASTER WELCOMES NEW GUARDIANS!

Today, the Guildmaster welcomed [insert the number of children in your club] new Guardians to Ancora. 'They all look very talented,' he said. 'And I'm looking forward to the stories they're going to find this week.'

BANANAS, ONIONS, JAM AND GRAVY NOW AVAILABLE IN THE GUILD DINING ROOM!

The Head of Feeding Faces is pleased to announce new dishes in the Guild Dining Room. Bananas, onions, raspberry jam and beef gravy are all now available. A special dessert has been created – bananas and onions covered with a layer of jam, all topped off with some delightful gravy. Delicious!

REPORTS OF LOTS OF NEW STORY-TREASURES

News is coming in of the locations of lots of new Ancoran story-treasures. It is hoped that Guardians will be able to find them and unlock some great new stories to add to the Saga. Which reminds me, I must find my spare robes. The last time I saw them, they were being used to strain vegetables in the Dining Room!

To start to equip the Guardians, the Shiner gives out a copy of the map of Ancora to each Company. (See the Treasure Store, page 96.) He checks that everyone has received at least one firebug, and explains that they are vital friends for Guardians: they light the way in dark places and a wise Guardian is never without a good supply. He boasts that his special Guardian skill is 'firebug whispering': he always has lanterns and firebugs galore – so he must be the wisest Guardian ever!

The Keeper and Kal say that now they will tell everyone about today's Quest.

TREASURE HUNT

As part of their training, on this first Quest, all the Guardians will get to go on the treasure hunt. Kal checks that each Company is equipped with backpacks, tools, firebugs and lanterns. The Elder Guardians should share out their lanterns and equipment with their Company. Kal leads the treasure hunt while the Keeper goes to the back, to make sure no one gets lost.

The hunt is based on the traditional 'Bear Hunt' game but has been adapted to follow the map of Ancora. Depending on your venue and the number of children, you may be able to move around while you go hunting or stay in one place and march on the spot. (Pre-empt any 11-year-olds thinking this is babyish by extra enthusiasm and exaggerating the words and actions.)

Kal leads, with everyone joining in as much as possible:

We're going on a treasure hunt,
We're gonna find a fine one.
What a beautiful day, we're not scared.

Uh-oh, grass! Long, wavy grass of Sabana.
We can't go over it, we can't go under it.
Oh, no! We've gotta go through it.
Swish-swash, swish-swash, swish-swash.

We're going...

Uh-oh, a waterfall! The high, high waterfall of Cascada.
We can't go over it, we can't go under it.
Oh, no! We've gotta go through it. Splash-splosh, splash-splosh, splash-splosh.
We're going...

Uh-oh, sand! The hot dunes of Anmos.
We can't go over it, we can't go under it.
Oh, no! We've gotta go through it. Whifft-whafft, whifft-whafft, whifft-whafft.
We're going...

Uh-oh, a forest! A big, frozen forest.
We can't go over it, we can't go under it.
Oh, no! We've gotta go through it. Shiver-slip, shiver-slip, shiver-slip.
We're going...

Uh-oh, a snowstorm!
A swirling, whirling snowstorm on the ice plains.
We can't go over it, we can't go under it.
Oh, no! We've gotta go through it. Hoo-woo, hoo-woo, hoo-woo.
We're going...

Uh-oh, a cave! A chilly, freezing ice cave.
We can't go over it, we can't go under it.
Oh, no! We've gotta go through it. Tiptoe, tiptoe, tiptoe... WHAT'S THAT?

Kal reaches behind a door or barrier (into the cave) and feels around in the 'darkenss', he says:

It's all stringy... There's lots of it.

It doesn't seem to be moving.

If I lean in, I can just reach it...

Kal topples behind the barrier and then passes out a pile of fishing nets, while trying to disentangle himself from them in the process. He reappears and declares:

IT'S THE TREASURE!

Then he realises the hunt has taken a long time and shouts, 'Time to go home.' Kal picks up the nets. Everyone turns round to hurry back to the Hall of Memory so now the Keeper takes over the lead:

QUICK! Before the firebugs fade!

Back through the ice cave, tiptoe, tiptoe.
Back through the snowstorm, over the ice plains, hoo-woo, hoo-woo.
Back through the frozen forest, shiver-slip, shiver-slip, shiver-slip.
Back through the hot sand dunes, whifft-whafft, whifft-whafft, whifft-whafft.
Back through the waterfall, splash-splosh, splash-splosh.
Back through the long grass, swish-swash, swish-swash.
Up through the city, step-step, step-step, step-step.
Get to the Great Door, creeeeak-creeeeak, creeeeak-creeeeak, thud.
Into the Hall of Memory, pad-pad, pad-pad, pad-pad.
Sit in our Companies.
We'll go on another treasure hunt next time!

Kal and the Keeper meet up; Kal gives her the treasure which she takes to her workstation. Kal explains that it is her job to check that the treasure is the real thing and to validate that it is the key to one of the stories of the Saga.

GUARDIANS SINGING

Introduce the Firebugs, the band (if you have one) and invite them to teach the **GUARDIANS OF ANCORA** holiday club theme song and any actions, if you've come up with some. Sing it a couple of times so that the Guardians begin to get the hang of it, rather than singing other songs at this point. Say that you'll sing it again later!

STORY OF THE SAGA

Fabula appears on stage alone and introduces herself. She explains she is the chief storyteller of Ancora and it is her job to make sure the stories of the Saga (the Bible) are told every day. The power of storytelling fuels the light of the Spire and shines throughout Ancora. Fabula is sad because many of the story-treasures are missing. The people of Ancora are determined to get them back so they can, once again, tell the stories that have been lost. More help is needed, and Fabula fears it will not be possible to find enough new Guardian recruits – which would mean the stories were lost for ever...

The Keeper appears, bringing the pile of fishing nets. Immediately, Fabula's mood changes and she becomes more animated as the Keeper explains that not only have all these new Guardians signed up (indicating the children) but they will be here throughout the club and seeking for lost Ancoran treasures every day. Fabula is eager to unlock the treasure hidden within the story-treasure and tell today's Story of the Saga…

Storytelling options

Each day, there are three options suggested for telling the Bible story: you can use the same approach each time, mix and match how you tell the story, or combine two or more approaches. Choose which will be most helpful for your team, your children and the style of your club.

I Fabula or another storyteller tells the story based on Luke 5:1–11 using their own words and personal storytelling style, if possible. You can use the section headings and ideas from the scripted version (see option III) as memory joggers and to vary your story presentation each time, if you wish.

II Introduce today's video storytelling episode available to download from the **GUARDIANS OF ANCORA** multimedia downloads page. (If you are telling the story and using the video, tell the story first, then show the video so the children already have the outline of the events before seeing the episode.)

III Or the storyteller may prefer to follow the fully scripted retold Bible story for Quest 1 on page 76.

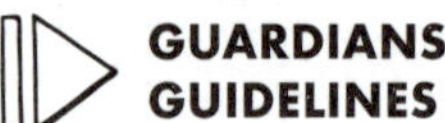

GUARDIANS' GUIDELINES

'Jesus said: Love the Lord your God with all your heart, soul and mind.'
Matthew 22:37

Before the day, prepare a set of large cards, with one word of the verse on each card. Also prepare a large chart with the days of the club down one side and space to record a daily time for each day. Be ready with a timer or stopwatch.

Invite children up to the front to take the daily *Learn and remember* challenge: you will need 14 children. They will each be given a card to hold and have to get themselves into the right order for the words of the verse. Before they start, explain that you will be timing how long it takes to sort out the words.

Give out the cards, face down, and with a three, two, one countdown, start the timer. See how long it takes for the children to line up in verse order. (The Firebugs could play an urgent rhythm to speed them along.) Involve everyone in encouraging them, making suggestions, cheering and so on. Stop the timer, announce the result and record it on the chart.

Read the words aloud. List a few things that love is not. For example, fluffy candyfloss, Valentine's cards, just being nice etc. Say that love is so much more – it requires everything that we are and all that we have. This verse is saying that when we love God we have to love him with all that we are and have. We'll be finding out how God will help us to love him and why he is worth loving in the first place.

All read the verse together. Then ask one or two children to turn their cards down and re-read the verse, filling in the gaps from memory. Repeat a few times, until about half the words are hidden. (Don't go on too long, for this first learning time.)

Use the *Learn and remember* verse song, 'God is Love', making your own actions to emphasise certain words such as 'love', 'heart', 'soul', 'strength'.

GUARDIANS' GOLD

Say that Jesus had a job for the fishermen to do, he called them to follow him and 'catch people' instead of fish. On the one hand it must have been very hard for the fishermen to drop everything and follow Jesus, but on the other hand there was obviously something about Jesus that the fishermen want to go with him.

Interview one of the Elder Guardians about a time when they were aware that Jesus called them to do something and how they responded. Was it easy? How did they know it was Jesus, and not just an idea they were making up? What does the story of the call of the fishermen and their willingness to follow Jesus mean to them? What is the 'treasure' in their relationship with Jesus?

UNLOCK THE TREASURE
⏱ 45 MINUTES IN SMALL GROUPS

VICTUALS

Make sure the children are comfortable in their Companies, as they settle for their refreshments. With younger children who can take longer over this, you may want to begin talking about the story as they drink their drinks.

TREASURE MAP: BIBLE DISCOVERY

With older children (8 to 11s)
Give the children a few minutes to complete the personal details on pages 1, 4 and 5 of *Guardian's Journal*. (Finish these pages in any Company time, if necessary.)

Ask whether anyone has ever had something really hard to do. How did they get on? Have a (lighthearted) personal example to share, if the children are reluctant to chat, at this early stage of the club. Say that today's **Story of the Saga** was about a group of men who faced lots of different challenges. Encourage the children to remember who the men were and what challenges they faced. Explain that they're going to look at these challenges a bit more, now. Read Luke 5:1–11 from *Guardian's Journal* page 7 or from a Bible. Pick out the words where Jesus tells Simon what to do (v 4); then find words where Jesus tells Simon not be afraid and calls him to follow him (v 10). Ask the children what they think it would have been like for Simon and the other fishermen when they heard Jesus speaking to them.

From the **Story of the Saga**, the children will know that after catching an enormous haul of fish the fishermen dropped their nets and followed Jesus. Look in a Bible atlas or *Guardian's Journal* page 9 to see where this story took place (Lake Galilee). Ask the children why they think the fishermen hadn't found any fish all night. What difference did listening to Jesus' directions make? Encourage the children to think about times when they don't know what to do, or feel like their plans have gone wrong. How might they be able to listen out for Jesus' voice guiding them in these times? Ask them how they feel about the idea that listening to Jesus' words brings blessing. (This idea will be picked up again in 'Benison'.)

Turn to Luke 5:1–11 (*Guardian's Journal* pages 7 and 8). In twos and threes, challenge the children to read the verses and see if they can find Simon Peter's response to Jesus. Ask why they think he responds the way he does. How would they have reacted? Encourage the children to say whether they would have dropped their nets and followed Jesus. Why, or why not?

Invite the children to read verse 10b (*Guardian's Journal* page 10) and write the words in the fish in the correct order or copy out the verse as a reminder that Jesus called the fishermen to follow him, and he calls us to follow him too.

Encourage everyone to think back to the personal examples you started with. What was hard for the fishermen and what was easy? Ask whether the children think they would have trusted Jesus as the fishermen did – and offer

your own answer. Encourage them to say how they feel about the idea that Jesus is calling them to follow him too.

With younger children (5 to 8s)
Give the children a few minutes to complete the personal details on page 4 of *Guardian's Stories*. (Finish these pages in any Company time, if necessary.)

Ask who the **Story of the Saga** was about today. Find out whether the children realise that the story of Jesus calling the fishermen is from the Bible. Find Luke 5:1–11 in a Bible or on page 6 of *Guardian's Stories* and read it aloud. Ask: 'What did Jesus ask the fishermen to do? Is that a surprising request? How would you have reacted?'

Invite a confident reader to read verses 4, 5 and 6, with everyone following the words in their Bible or booklets. Chat about the instructions that Jesus gave to Simon. Make sure the children notice that when Simon follows Jesus' instructions he is 'blessed' or receives good things. Say that they have already heard that when Jesus calls the fishermen to follow him they drop their nets and go with him, but how do they think the fishermen felt about leaving everything behind? What does Jesus say to the fishermen about this? Encourage them to look for the answer in verse 10 or sort out the puzzle on *Guardian's Stories* page 7.

Ask the children whether they are ever afraid of things. Perhaps some might be afraid of the dark, or afraid of spiders. Say that Jesus wants us to trust him when we are afraid and he wants to help us be less scared. Explain that there are some things that are dangerous and it is right to be 'afraid' of those things as it helps us to stay

safe. But there are other things that we are afraid of that won't actually hurt us. Invite the children to draw a simple picture of the thing(s) they are afraid of (that won't actually hurt them) and then invite them to write the name of 'Jesus' over their picture. If there are children in your group who are not confident writers allocate a colour to represent Jesus and invite them colour over their drawing with the 'Jesus' colour. Remind the children that Jesus wants us to trust him and that he is always with us when we are afraid.

Invite the children to sketch quick scenes of fishermen pulling very full nets out of the water into their boats; or complete the picture in *Guardian's Stories*. Ask why this happened. Because the fishermen did as Jesus told them!

Give an opportunity for spontaneous prayer by asking: 'What do you want to say to God?', and suggesting the children tell him now.

With all ages
Adapt these questions to suit your group, sharing your own feelings, opinions and experiences as appropriate (some are also in *Guardian's Journal* but are open-ended, with no right or wrong answer, so can be answered at any age):
⊕ What have you discovered that you didn't know before?
⊕ Has this story reminded you of anything you already knew?
⊕ What do you want to think about some more?
⊕ What are the fishermen like in this story? Can you think of three words to describe them?
⊕ How are the characters in this story like you or someone you know?
⊕ What's your favourite part of the story?
⊕ What have you learnt about Jesus

from today's story?

ORISON
Bring along a large piece of fishing net and enough pieces of ribbon for one per child in your Company.

Say that, just as Jesus called the fishermen to follow him, he calls us to follow him too. Explain to the children that if they would like to find out more about following Jesus then they can choose a ribbon and tie it on to the net. Remember that the children in your group will all be at a different stage in their faith journey. Pass the ribbons around the group; invite each child either to choose a ribbon and tie it to the net, as a symbol of their desire to find out more about Jesus, or simply pass the ribbons to the next person. Some younger children may need some gentle help to affix their ribbons to the net. Pray for all the children in your group, asking God's blessing upon them.

CONSTRUCTION
Choose a construction activity from the **Treasure Store** pages 80 to 83. There are craft ideas based on the **GUARDIANS OF ANCORA** theme and on the Bible teaching. Today's Bible construction is 'Fishing nets' on page 80.

For extra craft ideas, see *Ultimate Craft* (SU 978 1 84427 364 5).

GAMES
Help the Guardians shape up by choosing suitable games from pages 84 to 86. There are extra themed games at the **GUARDIANS OF ANCORA** multimedia downloads area. For even more games ideas see *Ultimate Games* (SU 978 1 84427 365 2).

GUARDIANS' GATHERING
🕐 25 MINUTES ALL TOGETHER

TREASURE CHEST
Welcome everyone back together by playing the **GUARDIANS OF ANCORA** theme song. If there are any messages in the **Treasure Chest**, read one or two out. As this is the first Quest, there may not be many jokes, messages, pictures and questions, apart from those the team has produced in advance or the children have written or drawn during the session, so you might want to have a couple up your sleeve. Encourage children to bring their contributions, jokes and pictures tomorrow.

COMPANY SHOWCASE

Choose a Company and invite the Elder Guardian and two or three of the children to come to the front to show everyone something they have been doing in their **Company duties**. It might be an item they have made to decorate their space, an emblem or flag they have devised or a motto to say. Admire what they have shown and thank them for being enthusiastic Guardians.

THE SEARCH FOR THE GOLDEN SHIELD

Introduce the drama, set in the world of Ancora. For children who were not at Service 1, give a brief recap (the drama is designed to work for children who have not seen the Service 1 episode).

Today, the new Guardians receive their first quest, but where will it send them? Like the fishermen, they're about to embark on a long journey and they don't know exactly where they will end up – but they have a **Treasure Map** to guide them! The super-confident and heroic Swift launches her career as a Guardian, knowing she will be the best ever. But there are signs that there may be trouble ahead and that perhaps being sure of herself and saying she is brave may not be enough…

KEEPER'S QUESTIONS

Divide the children into evenly-matched teams and devise a quiz that relates to all that has happened so far. This can include facts about Ancora, as well as facts from the stories and the *Learn and remember* verse.

Alternatively, you can use the quiz from page 100 or from the **GUARDIANS OF ANCORA** multimedia downloads area based on the Bible story from Quest 1.

BENISON

Ask if anyone noticed what happened when the fishermen in the Bible story today lowered their nets where Jesus told them to. They caught a huge number of fish, even though they had spent hours fishing earlier and caught nothing. When we do as Jesus asks us he will give us good things.

Give each child a fish shape and invite them to decorate it using felt-tip pens. Encourage them to write on the reverse of the fish one or two words (or draw a simple picture or symbol) about the good things in their lives.

Play the melody of a worship song and encourage the children to say thank you to God for the things on their fish.

REVIVE!

The Firebugs lead the children in a couple of lively songs.

Round off **Guardians' gathering** by asking two children to say in one sentence what one thing they will share when they get home. Children are used to doing this in school. Elder Guardians can ask a similar question when the children are back in their Companies.

Kal reminds everyone about the collection procedure, and assures them that he is looking forward to seeing them at the next Quest. Where will the treasure be hidden and what will it be? What story will be unlocked by the treasure map? How will Swift get on in the drama tomorrow?

Sing the **GUARDIANS OF ANCORA** holiday club theme song one more time and then send the children back to their Companies.

SIGNING OFF

🕐 10 MINUTES IN SMALL GROUPS

Chat with the children about the 'special Guardian skills' that you identified earlier in the day during **Company duties** (or work out what they are, now). If feasible, have each child demonstrate or mime their skill to the others.

RESTORATION: CLEARING UP AND A QUICK DEBRIEF

Once the children have gone, tidy up and do any necessary preparation for the following day. As many as possible in the team should meet to debrief on how the first day has gone, and identify any hitches that could be put right or any children who have been unhappy. Report back on how children and leaders in each Company have settled and pray together.

Remember to acknowledge and affirm team members' contributions to the session. If possible, share a meal together (although you may only wish to do that on the last day).

USING THE **GUARDIANS OF ANCORA** APP WITH THIS QUEST

If you have access to a tablet and are able to download the **GUARDIANS OF ANCORA** app there are several ways you could use this to enhance today's quest.

- ⊕ If you are able to connect your tablet to a projector, you could play through relevant parts of 'Jesus and the fishermen' as a way of introducing the story to the children.
- ⊕ If you have enough tablets to have one per company you could encourage children to take it turns playing through 'Jesus and the fishermen' at appropriate points in your programme. You might like to set a time limit to make sure everyone gets a turn.

If you have enough tablets for one company to have one each, you could incorporate time during construction or games for companies to rotate and play through 'Jesus and the fishermen' in a dedicated 'tablet zone' under supervision. You could suggest the following to the children:

- ⊕ As a new Guardian, listen to Fabula the storyteller who will show you what to do.
- ⊕ Find your way to the shore of the lake and see what is going on.
- ⊕ See if you can follow the fishermen, even though you don't have a boat.

If you don't have access to a tablet, and aren't able to download the **GUARDIANS OF ANCORA** app yourself, don't worry, there are still plenty of exciting ways to engage with **GUARDIANS OF ANCORA**. You can start by visiting www.guardiansofancora.com to find out more!

Remember to encourage the children who attend your group to download the app for themselves if they have access to a tablet at home.

QUEST 11
JESUS HEALS THE ROMAN OFFICER'S SERVANT

KEY PASSAGE
Luke 7:1–10

KEY STORYLINES
⊕ The Guardians find a pair of Roman sandals, which launch the story of the Roman officer's servant.
⊕ The Roman officer's servant is extremely unwell and about to die. The officer demonstrates great faith in Jesus and his servant is healed.
⊕ Faith in Jesus, his authority and power is all that is needed for the servant to be healed.

KEY AIMS
⊕ To welcome each child to the club and remind them of what has happened so far.
⊕ To find out that Jesus is God's Son and has his authority and power.
⊕ To identify that having faith in Jesus can have amazing results.
⊕ To have a growing sense of excitement and wonder about finding the story-treasures.

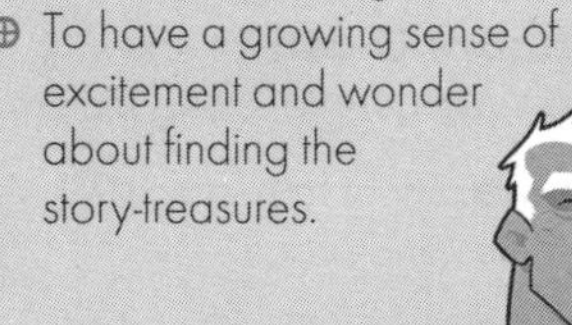

GUARDIANS BACKGROUND

NO CHURCH BACKGROUND
Explain that the Romans were occupying Israel and that normally there was hatred and distrust on both sides. However, as well as limited medicine available from doctors and herbalists, it was very common for people (Romans and Jews) to use religious practices to seek healing. Emphasise how unusual it was for a Roman officer to show so much care for a servant, and also to have such a respectful relationship with the Jews. It wasn't unexpected for Jewish people to ask one of their teachers to pray for healing, but it was very rare for a foreigner to do so. Jesus is amazed that the Roman officer recognises the authority Jesus has; even at a distance, if Jesus commands healing, then it will happen. At this point no one else had recognised Jesus could do that.

CHURCH CHILDREN
Church children are likely to know that it was Romans who executed Jesus. They may expect all Romans to be 'baddies', so make sure you emphasise that God loved the Romans as much as he loved the Jews. God would respond to their prayers if they had faith in him. It might be worth asking the children if they know other stories of healing from the Old Testament to help them understand that, when Jesus went around healing people, he was doing something God had always done. They may ask about healing today, and it is worth reminding them that Jesus is the same 'yesterday, today and forever'. God has always been able to act at a distance. However, that does not mean every prayer is answered in the way we would like.

WITH OTHER FAITHS
Jewish children may know the Old Testament stories mentioned above and that God is sometimes 'God our healer'. Jewish people commonly use words from the Psalms when they pray for healing. Despite believing in a non-interventionist god, many Muslims also commonly pray for healing when sick, as do Hindus and Buddhists. Sometimes there are ritual ways of praying. Use of 'medicine men' is also common in animistic faiths. It may be helpful to explain the context of the then animosity between Romans and Jews (occupier and occupied) as one of the surprising elements of the story, and also the surprise that it was the foreigner who first recognised the scope of Jesus' authority.

WITH ADDITIONAL NEEDS
Many of the stories this week are about healing. For some children with disabilities or additional needs, this may be an issue that needs handling sensitively. Faith could be a difficult concept to understand. You might want to begin at a very simple level, using the phrase: 'Believing that God can help me with difficult things'. Learn the Makaton or BSL sign for 'faith' or 'believe' to help reinforce understanding. Be aware some children with physical difficulties may find action songs hard. Chat with them and find ways to make these songs accessible and just as enjoyable. Remember that not all disabilities are obvious – some with ADHD or dyspraxia will struggle to coordinate the faster, more complicated actions.

ELDER **GUARDIANS** GATHER

SPIRITUAL PREPARATION

Read Luke 7:1–10 together.

Say that today's passage reveals the Roman officer's faith in Jesus. The officer hadn't even met Jesus, only heard about him, and yet he still chose to believe that Jesus had the power to heal his servant.

Invite everyone to consider their own faith and how easy they find it to trust in God. Encourage a few people to share what trusting God a little more might look like. Challenge everyone to think about how the example of their faith will affect the children attending the club, and how they might be feeling about their own faith journeys.

Then pray for the children in your groups by name, especially any with difficulties or who seemed hard to engage with. Pray as well that any newcomers will quickly feel welcome and become part of their group. Pray for the team members, especially anyone who seems unwell or tired!

PRACTICAL PREPARATION

Talk through your programme together. Remind everyone about the key learning aims and who is doing what, ensuring that everyone knows their part in the day and has everything they need. Pay particular attention to younger team members or those who have not been involved before and may be feeling a bit uncertain. Encourage them over the course of the session. This may be the role of the overall leader or could be assigned to another member of the team, or member of the church whose sole role is to encourage the team. Create an atmosphere so that people feel able to ask about anything they are not 100 per cent clear about.

Set up the different areas of the club and make sure that everything is in place in plenty of time, so you are ready as the first children come from the registration area. You will need to hide the *Learn and remember* word cards around your venue ready for 'Guardians' guidelines'. Leaders need to be especially welcoming to parents and children who have not been before or any adults accompanying children who look uncomfortable being in a church setting. As this is the second day, most people will know what the format is so will be more relaxed.

Give one of each pair of shoes for 'Treasure hunt', including one 'Roman' sandal, to members of the team: they should keep the shoes with them, but discreetly. Make sure everyone knows what to say during the activity.

Listen to any last-minute information or instructions from the Guildmaster, Keeper or Kal, or from the drama, music or refreshment team. Remind the team to set an example of joining in and responding to prompts from the upfront presenters: this will encourage the children to get more involved.

WHAT-YOU-NEED CHECKLIST

- **Registration:** registration forms, badges, labels, pens, team lists, paper firebugs
- **Guardians assemble:** the Keeper's keys, a selection of Hall of Memory decorations
- **Ancora Herald:** today's news, a peach
- **Treasure hunt:** nine pairs of shoes, a pair of 'Roman' sandals, an empty box, a lantern glowing blue
- **Music:** Firebugs band or backing tracks
- **Story of the Saga:** pair of 'Roman' sandals from 'Treasure hunt', story script, **GUARDIANS OF ANCORA** multimedia story downloads
- **Guardians' guidelines:** verse cards, time chart, timer
- **Victuals:** drinks and snack
- **Treasure map:** Bibles, *Guardian's Journals* or *Guardian's Stories*, art materials
- **Orison:** wall or board, art materials, cover-up and clean-up facilities
- **Construction:** materials for your chosen craft option(s)
- **Games:** equipment for your chosen game option(s)
- **Treasure Chest:** for jokes, messages, questions and pictures
- **Drama:** script from page 90, costumes and props
- **Keeper's questions:** quiz questions
- **Benison:** a Bible

THE SECOND **QUEST**

COMPANY DUTIES
🕐 10 MINUTES

If you have new children, introduce them to one another; make sure they all know they belong to your small group: the Company of ——s and teach them the motto. Use it straight away as a password, to reinforce the sense of belonging.

Remind the children about the **Treasure Chest** so they can add any items they have brought or write and draw something now.

Make sure everyone was given a (paper) firebug as they came in. Chat about the previous holiday club Quest and respond to comments and questions. Give some hints about today's Quest, to raise the children's expectations. You could practise the *Learn and remember* verse together, too.

In any time remaining, continue decorating your Company space, making it unique to your group of children.

GUARDIANS ASSEMBLE
🕐 45 MINUTES ALL TOGETHER

Once all the children are settled in the Hall of Memory, the Keeper of the Keys and Kal re-introduce themselves and then re-introduce Fabula and the Shiner (if you are featuring them).

Welcome the Guardians again, especially any new children today. See what they can remember about Ancora and why it is so important to have plenty of Guardians for the Hall of Memory.

The Keeper of the Keys explains more about her role in the city, looking after the most amazing museum-library-gallery ever. She can move around the room, showing some of the themed decorations and briefly explaining what they are (for example, the fishing nets from Quest 1, an old book), ending with her bunch of keys. They remind her of all sorts of things: they open the doors and cupboards in the Hall of Memory (always useful!); they are a symbol of the keys to all the knowledge of and about Ancora and the Saga; and they remind her of a story from the Saga when Peter realises that Jesus is God's Son and Jesus says 'I will give you the keys to the kingdom of heaven...' (Matthew 16:19).

Kal breaks into her talk and says that now it's time to tell the Guardians about today's Quest. But there's another interruption as the Shiner arrives with news of the city. (If you are not using this character, have the 'news' arrive as a message for one of the presenters to read out.)

ANCORA HERALD
The Shiner performs this script:

Here are the stories from Ancora!
Listen if you're an explorer!
Take note and memorise my speech
Or you'll turn into a peach!

He produces a peach from his robes, then gives it to the Keeper. As he reads the headlines, he shouts the words in capitals, as if he were a newspaper vendor on the street.

GUARDIANS EXCEL IN TRAINING

Congratulations go to [Insert Company name here] **and** [Insert another Company name here] **who did very well in Guardian training yesterday! They** [talk about what both companies did well]. **However, the Guildmaster wants to tell all the Guardians that he's very impressed with everyone!**

MARKET DAY IN ANCORA!

Ancora's market place will be full of people today as stall holders try to entice customers. Stalls include Strictly Comb Dancing, where you can buy brushes and hair care products; the X Factor, which sells X-rays, xylophones and anything else beginning with X; and You've Been Framed for all you need for painting and photography!

STORY-TREASURE FOUND

Yesterday, Guardians found a new story-treasure. A pile of fishing nets helped us all to discover the story of Jesus calling the fishermen! That reminds me, I must remember to go fishing later. I've almost run out of lettuce!

Kal and the Keeper say that now they will tell everyone about today's Quest.

TREASURE HUNT
The Keeper produces a box labelled 'SHOES' (which contains the matching shoes from the pairs you split up earlier, apart from the 'Roman' sandal, which the Keeper has hidden about her person). She explains that Elder Guardians and Apprentice Elders love swapping shoes from the Hall of Memory, but sometimes forget to bring them back. There are ten shoes missing: will the Guardians help her find them?

The Keeper asks for volunteers to form teams of twos and threes, then removes one shoe at a time from the box. One team at a time visits one of the Elder Guardians or Apprentice Elders (ask them all to stand, wherever they are in the room, including those without shoes) and says: 'We're seeking a shoe that has [describe their shoe] for the Hall of Memory.' If the Elder Guardian doesn't have a shoe at all, they say: 'Sorry, I can't help.' If they have a different shoe, they say: 'No, but I know about [describe their shoe].' The team keeps asking Elder Guardians until they find and collect the right shoe, and take it to the Keeper. The finders wait on the stage with the shoe, while another team seeks the next shoe.

When the nine shoes have been found, the Keeper (with help from the rest of the club) counts them and realises there's one still missing. She pats her pockets until she finds the last shoe, the 'Roman' sandal. Then she says, 'This shoe looks very old, in fact it almost looks Roman to me.' She seems baffled and asks the whole club if they have any ideas what kind of person might once have owned this shoe. Once she has the answer 'A Roman soldier/officer', the team member harbouring the matching sandal suddenly 'finds' it about their person and takes it to the Keeper.

The Keeper is pleased to have so many shoes returned and is busy thanking everyone; but Kal is bouncing with excitement. By collecting these shoes together, the Guardians have found a story-treasure! He proves it by showing his firebug lantern: the light is blue! Isn't that what the Shiner said might happen? The Keeper is not sure ('Oh, no it isn't') so Kal enrols the support of the Guardians: 'Oh, yes it is!' Eventually, the Keeper gives way and agrees to take the story-treasure to Fabula.

GUARDIANS SINGING
The Firebugs remind the children of the **GUARDIANS OF ANCORA** holiday club theme song and sing it again.

Add other songs, mostly repeating those from yesterday, but perhaps introducing one new one. If some children already know a song, invite them to come out and help teach it to the others, especially if it has actions or dance movements.

STORY OF THE SAGA

Fabula comes on stage alone and interacts with the children, asking if it's true that they have signed up as Guardians and if they have really come to help seek and recover the missing artefacts from the Hall of Memory. It's not that Fabula doubts them, exactly – but it seems almost too good to be true. The stories of the Saga mean so much to Fabula and she has been so sad to lose many of them. Is it possible that the Guardians have found another story-treasure today?

While the children are answering, the Keeper comes in, bringing the box of shoes. Fabula takes it easily and is so pleased to see such treasure that she doesn't seem to notice the weight. The Keeper is puzzled: the treasure didn't seem very *exciting* to her. Fabula suggests she listens and finds out.

Storytelling options

Each day, there are three options suggested for telling the Bible story: you can use the same approach each time, mix and match how you tell the story, or combine two or more approaches. Choose which will be most helpful for your team, your children and the style of your club.

I   Fabula or another storyteller tells the story based on Luke 7:1–10 using their own words and personal storytelling style, if possible. You can use the section headings and ideas from the scripted version (see option III) as memory joggers and to vary your story presentation each time, if you wish.

II   Introduce today's video storytelling episode available to download from the **GUARDIANS OF ANCORA** multimedia downloads page. (If you are telling the story and using the video, tell the story first, then show the video so the children already have the outline of the events before seeing the episode.)

III   Or the storyteller may prefer to follow the fully scripted retold Bible story for Quest 2 on pages 76 and 77.

GUARDIANS' GUIDELINES

'Jesus said: Love the Lord your God with all your heart, soul and mind.'
Matthew 22:37

Remember to provide lots of opportunities for children individually and as a group to demonstrate that they have learnt the verse, with a suitable reward.

Before the session, hide the word cards (from Quest 1) around the room, or give them to the team members to hold. Choose one Company and send those Guardians off to find the words and bring them back to you. (Make the finding fairly easy, so this doesn't slow down the pace of the club too much.)

Thank the Company when they have found all the words and then call another set of children to the stage to take the daily *Learn and remember* challenge: you will need 14 children. Before they start, explain that you will be timing how long it takes to get themselves into the right order for the words of the verse.

Give out the cards, face down, and with a three, two, one countdown, start the timer. See how long it takes for the children to line up in verse order. (The Firebugs could play an urgent rhythm to speed them along.) Involve everyone in encouraging them, making suggestions, cheering and so on. Stop the timer, announce the result and record it on the chart (hopefully, not as long as before!).

Say that God loves us very much and calls us to love him in return.

Sing the *Learn and remember* verse song a couple of times, using the actions you've created.

GUARDIANS' GOLD

Interview an older leader who has known Jesus as a friend for years and years. Ask them how old they were when they first realised that they were Jesus' friend and had become his follower. What has been easy about following Jesus? What has been hard? Would they recommend it? What does this story of Jesus healing the Roman officer's servant mean to them? What is the 'treasure' in their relationship with Jesus?

UNLOCK THE TREASURE
🕐 45 MINUTES IN SMALL GROUPS

VICTUALS

Make sure the children are comfortable in their Companies, as they settle for their refreshments. Younger children can take longer over this, so you may want to begin talking about the story as they drink their drinks.

TREASURE MAP: BIBLE DISCOVERY

With older children (8 to 11s)

Give any new children a few minutes to complete the personal details on pages 1, 4 and 5 of their *Guardian's Journal*. (Finish these pages in any Company time, if necessary.)

Ask whether anyone can think of anything that needs 'power' to work. Challenge them to point out items around your **GUARDIANS OF ANCORA** holiday club space that need power. If the children need prompting, mention things like the lights, or maybe some of the instruments in the band, maybe a phone or television/projector… Ask where the power comes from.

Encourage the children to think back to the **Story of the Saga**: what sort of power is described? Ask how they feel about Jesus being powerful.

Encourage the children to find page 15 in their *Guardian's Journals* or Luke 7 in Bibles. Say that the army officer in the story would probably have been a Roman soldier. As a Roman, this man would normally have been well known and respected, but he might not have been very popular among the Jews.

Invite the children to think of a reason why the Roman officer turned to Jesus. What did Jesus say about the officer's faith? How might the officer have been feeling? What does it really mean to have faith in Jesus? Some children may need a little help to understand the concept of faith. You might find words such as 'trust', 'belief' and 'hope' helpful in your conversation.

Encourage the children to say whether they think it is easy to put faith in Jesus. Ask what makes it hard.

Say that the Roman officer had faith in Jesus' power. Invite everyone to turn to *Guardian's Journal* page 18 to find Luke 7:7b. Even the words of Jesus have great power to change things. Ask if anyone can remember any other words of Jesus – things he said to those he met, or things he said about himself. Invite the children to turn to page 18 in *Guardian's Journal* to find a selection of other powerful words of Jesus.

Explain that, because the Roman officer had great faith in Jesus' power, it meant that he turned to Jesus in his time of need. Encourage the children to think about the problems they face and how they might be able to turn to Jesus for help in these situations. (Be sensitive to the circumstances of the children in your group as you discuss these questions.)

With younger children (5 to 8s)
Give any new children a few minutes to complete the personal details on page 4 of *Guardian's Stories*. (Finish these pages in any Company time, if necessary.)

Sensitively chat about what happens in our homes, school and wider community when someone is unwell or poorly. What happens to help people get better? It is probably wise to keep the tone of this conversation as light as possible, giving examples such as getting a cold or grazing a knee, unless you feel other examples are more appropriate. Ease the conversation into asking about today's **Story of the Saga**. Ask whether the children realise that the story of the Roman officer's servant is from the Bible. Find Luke 7:1–10 on page 10 of *Guardian's Stories*, or in a Bible, and read it aloud, with the children following the words (in *Guardian's Stories*, these have been trimmed for younger readers). Work together to find out what happened in the story, paying particular attention to the words of Jesus.

Say: 'I wonder why Jesus said that he had not found faith like the Roman officer's for miles around'. See how the children respond: at this age, they may find it tricky to comprehend 'faith' and trying to describe it in too much detail could be confusing. On the other hand, they may find it straightforward to put faith in Jesus, exhibiting little or no doubt and having few questions.

Summarise the story by saying that because Jesus is God's Son he is very powerful, so powerful that he made a man who was very ill well again. Say that Jesus also commented on how good it was that the Roman officer had such a strong 'faith'. If you are using *Guardian's Stories*, find the words on page 12 (*Jesus can do amazing things!*); help the children to read the words and trace the shapes of the letters then invite them to decorate the page as they wish.

Alternatively, or in addition, you may wish to set out paper and art materials and work in twos or threes to create posters to show how amazing Jesus is, perhaps illustrating the miracle of healing from today's story.

With all ages
Adapt these questions to suit your group, sharing your own feelings, opinions and experiences as appropriate (some are also in *Guardian's Journal* but are open-ended, with no right or wrong answer, so can be answered at any age):
⊕ What have you discovered that you didn't know before?
⊕ Has this story reminded you of anything you already knew?
⊕ What do you want to think about some more?
⊕ How are the characters in this story like you or someone you know?
⊕ What have you learnt about God from today's story?
⊕ Do you ever find it hard to put your faith in Jesus? Do you think God can help you with this?
⊕ Do you think God will help you, when you ask him? How might he help?

ORISON
Prepare a large board or area of wall where the children can write or draw their responses to God as a street art wall. Depending on your situation, this could involve spray paints and stencils, brushes and paint or (cleaner to handle and easier to manage, with a group of children) thick felt-tip pens or chunky crayons. If you can go outside, brushing water on a blank wall is exciting and effective – and doesn't need cleaning afterwards! Make sure the area is at a suitable height for the children and large enough for them to work together. Have appropriate cover-up and clean-up equipment for your chosen materials. (You may find it helps to lay the board on the floor and all kneel around it to work; then stand the board up to display.)

You may wish to give the children some prompts for praying: mention the Bible discoveries you have just made and summarise what you've been finding out together. But remember it can be liberating for children to make their own spontaneous and natural responses: a 'street art wall' is a creative space for such expressions as it encourages inventiveness, scale and freedom. The act of marking their response on the 'wall' is a prayer in itself, but you may also like to summarise at the end with a spoken sentence and a shared 'Amen'.

USING THE
GUARDIANS OF ANCORA
APP WITH THIS QUEST

If you have access to a tablet and are able to download the **GUARDIANS OF ANCORA** app there are several ways you could use this to enhance today's quest.
⊕ If you are able to connect your tablet to a projector, you could play through relevant parts of 'Jesus and the Roman officer' as a way of introducing the story to the children.
⊕ If you have enough tablets to have one per company you could encourage children to take it turns playing through 'Jesus and the Roman officer' at appropriate points in your programme. You might like to set a time limit to make sure everyone gets a turn.

If you have enough tablets for one company to have one each, you could incorporate time during construction or games for companies to rotate and play through 'Jesus and the Roman officer' in a dedicated 'tablet zone' under supervision. You could suggest the following to the children:
⊕ Use your Guardian climbing and jumping skills to find the way through Capernaum.
⊕ Find the Roman officer, without being seen by the Roman guards.
⊕ Don't miss what Jesus is doing.

If you don't have access to a tablet, and aren't able to download the **GUARDIANS OF ANCORA** app yourself, don't worry, there are still plenty of exciting ways to engage with **GUARDIANS OF ANCORA**. You can start by visiting www.guardiansofancora.com to find out more!

Remember to encourage the children who attend your group to download the app for themselves if they have access to a tablet at home.

CONSTRUCTION

Choose a construction activity from the **Treasure Store** pages 80 to 83. There are craft ideas based on the **GUARDIANS OF ANCORA** theme and on the Bible teaching. Today's Bible construction is 'Sandals' on page 80.

For extra craft ideas, see *Ultimate Craft* (SU 978 1 84427 364 5).

GAMES

Help the Guardians shape up by choosing suitable games from pages 84 to 86. There are extra themed games at the **GUARDIANS OF ANCORA** multimedia downloads area. For even more games ideas see *Ultimate Games* (SU 978 1 84427 365 2).

GUARDIANS' GATHERING
🕐 25 MINUTES ALL TOGETHER

TREASURE CHEST

Welcome everyone back together by playing the **GUARDIANS OF ANCORA** theme song. Edit the contributions in the Treasure Chest today so that you read out the better jokes and messages and answer any important questions. Thank all the contributing Guardians and encourage them to bring more of their jokes, questions, messages and pictures tomorrow.

COMPANY SHOWCASE

Choose a Company and invite the Elder Guardian and two or three of the children to the front to show everyone something they have been doing in their 'Company duties'. It might be an item they have made to decorate their space, an emblem or flag they have devised or a motto to say. Admire what they have shown and thank them for being enthusiastic Guardians.

THE SEARCH FOR THE GOLDEN SHIELD

Recap on yesterday's adventure, for anyone who missed the session, and say that now it's time for the next episode of *The Search for the Golden Shield*. Today, Swift and Dash set out on their quest, but Swift isn't sure she has learnt enough and begins to worry that things will go wrong. Swift begins to doubt herself and to question what it means to be a **GUARDIAN OF ANCORA**.

KEEPER'S QUESTIONS

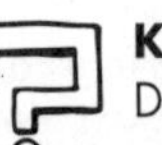

Divide the children into evenly-matched teams and devise a quiz that relates to all that has happened during your **GUARDIANS OF ANCORA** holiday club so far. This can include funny events that happened unique to your club (show images on the screen if you have been making a photographic record), as well as facts from the stories and the *Learn and remember* verse.

Alternatively, you can use the quiz from page 101 or from the **GUARDIANS OF ANCORA** multimedia downloads area based on the Bible story from Quest 2.

BENISON

Give a very brief summary of everything you have been discovering today: how the Roman officer put his faith in Jesus and how Jesus had the power and authority to heal the servant even from afar. Explain that there's a lot more in the Bible about the amazing things that Jesus did and about how to be one of his followers – and you're going to use some Bible words for your all-together prayer time now.

Find Psalm 117 and say it has the title 'Come praise the Lord!': teach the children this phrase as a response line to say in unison. Invite everyone to join in the prayer: say that you will read a line and then everyone should join in with the response.

REVIVE!

The Firebugs lead the children in a couple of lively songs.

Round off **Guardians' gathering** by asking two children to say in one sentence what one thing they will share when they get home. Children are used to doing this in school. Elder Guardians can ask a similar question when the children are back in their Companies.

The Keeper of the Keys reminds everyone about the collection procedure, and assures them that she is looking forward to seeing them the next day. Where will the story-treasure be hidden and what will it be? What story will be unlocked? Will Swift ever find the treasure she is seeking?

Sing the **GUARDIANS OF ANCORA** theme song one more time and then send the children back to their Companies.

SIGNING OFF
🕐 10 MINUTES IN SMALL GROUPS

Go round the group and ask each person to say what their 'special Guardian skill' is. Ask if anyone has used their skill since you met last time: what did they do?

RESTORATION: CLEARING UP AND A QUICK DEBRIEF

Once the children have gone, tidy up and do any necessary preparation for the following day. As many as possible in the team should meet to debrief on how the day has gone, identify any hitches that could be put right or any children who have been unhappy, report back on how children and leaders in each Company have been today and spend time praying together.

Remember to acknowledge and affirm team members' contributions to the session. If possible, share a meal together (although you may only wish to do that on the last day).

QUEST III
JESUS HEALS A WOMAN AND A GIRL

KEY PASSAGE
Luke 8:40-56

KEY STORYLINES
⊕ The Guardians find a collection of handprints, which release the story of Jairus' daughter and the woman who touched Jesus' coat.
⊕ The woman who touched Jesus' coat has been unwell for 12 years and no one has been able to heal her. Her faith in Jesus combined with his power to heal means that only one touch of his coat is enough to restore her to health.
⊕ The people claim that Jairus' daughter is dead, but Jesus is able to restore her to life.

KEY AIMS
⊕ To welcome each child to the club and remind them of everything that has happened so far.
⊕ To find out that even though Jesus is very powerful he is still interested in the detail of our lives.
⊕ To understand that Jesus has great compassion on those who are unwell or in need, and that he calls those who follow him to have the same compassion.
⊕ To create a mood of anticipation about Quest 4, in which Jesus performs another exciting miracle and reveals a little more of who he is.

GUARDIANS BACKGROUND

NO CHURCH BACKGROUND
The synagogue was the place where Jews worshipped when they were not at the Temple in Jerusalem. Jairus was an important man in the town. In those days, girls and women were seen as worth less than men and boys, in both Roman and Jewish cultures. Some people would have seen it as a waste of time for Jesus to heal a girl. In Jewish culture, there were times when women were deemed 'unclean' and they could not go out in public. One of those times was if the woman was bleeding (usually her period). For this woman to risk going out into the crowd, and even more, to touch Jesus' coat, was a brave thing. Her trust in God was great enough to overcome the potential embarrassment and rejection.

CHURCH CHILDREN
This group may know other healing stories about Jesus. Encourage them to share. Ask them to think about why it was brave for the woman to seek healing (she should not have been out in public, she had been ill for such a long time, everyone was likely to know her problem – there was a big chance for rejection). Draw the parallel between the age of Jairus' daughter and how long the woman had been ill. Jairus' daughter is about to become a woman in Jewish understanding, but the other woman has been ill as long as the girl had been alive! Emphasise that the girl's spirit returns to her – we are more than just body and mind. It is because we are spiritual beings that we can have a relationship with God rather than blindly worship in the way the rest of creation does.

WITH OTHER FAITHS
Although Muslims may expect that God can heal, there is no expectation of resuscitation or resurrection. It may be important to emphasise that the girl really was dead and really did come back to life. For those from faiths believing in reincarnation, such as Hinduism or Buddhism, it will be important to emphasise that this is the same spirit returning to the same body, not a reborn spirit in another body. Take seriously any questions the children ask about how this happened and what the relationship is between faith ('your faith has healed you'/'have faith, your daughter will be well') and answered prayer, especially if they have prayed and not been answered in the way they wished. It does not mean their faith was too small or that they were too imperfect.

WITH ADDITIONAL NEEDS
Making and wearing a special coat would be a useful multi-sensory tool today. It will help with hearing the story, and in opening up many aspects of it: this could be talking about Jesus' care while feeling safely wrapped up in the coat and then finding ways to help others feel the same. The Orison prayer activity is a helpful way to re-enforce the teaching, but it is good to remember that many children with additional needs are fearful of balloons. You may want to do the same activity, but using a picture of a balloon instead. Because of today's story, try to be aware of children struggling with bereavement, or those who have life-limiting disorders and their siblings.

ELDER **GUARDIANS** GATHER

The writer of Hebrews urges his readers to 'not neglect to meet together' (10:25) and, midway into the club, that's a timely reminder. You and the children may be in the swing of things now and, as those relationships build, there may be more opportunities to share the love of Jesus. Spend a few moments with God, before launching into another busy session.

SPIRITUAL PREPARATION

Read Luke 8:40–56 together.

Jesus performs another two incredible miracles – healing two women, both in desperate situations. Encourage everyone to try to imagine how the father of the sick girl might have felt or to consider the feelings of the woman who touched Jesus' coat, and to notice Jesus' compassionate response to both situations. Challenge them to reflect on the details of their own lives and know that God takes great care and interest in all that they are and do. Invite two or three team members to share a few thoughts.

Ask a few people to lead prayers for the following:
⊕ Pray for a deep desire to know, love and serve God as he deserves.
⊕ Think about how you can do that serving the children today. Lift each one to God in prayer and think about how they need blessing.
⊕ Pray today for God's power to be at work in the lives of the children, enabling them to understand and grasp his love for them.
⊕ Pray for the team, especially those running different activities or sessions.
⊕ Pray that you will see evidence of God at work in other ways too.

PRACTICAL PREPARATION

Talk through your programme together. Remind everyone about the key learning aims and who is doing what, ensuring that everyone knows their part in the day and has everything they need. Create an atmosphere in which people feel able to ask about anything they are not 100 per cent clear about.

Set up the different areas of the club and make sure that everything is in place in plenty of time, so you are ready as the first children come from the registration area. Leaders need to be especially welcoming to parents and children who have not been before or any adults accompanying children who look uncomfortable being in a church setting. As this is the third day, most people will know what the format is so will be more relaxed.

Listen to any last-minute information or instructions from the Guildmaster, Keeper or Kal, or from the drama, music or refreshment team. By now the children are likely to be joining in willingly and noisily: remind the team to keep an eye out for those who may be keeping on the fringe and those who may be getting over-excited.

WHAT-YOU-NEED CHECKLIST

☐ **Registration:** registration forms, badges, labels, pens, team lists, paper firebugs

☐ **Guardians' assemble:** towel and 'damaged gadget' for Kal

☐ **Ancora Herald:** today's news, butter

☐ **Treasure hunt:** a framed collection of hand prints, envelopes with clues

☐ **Music:** Firebugs band or backing tracks

☐ **Story of the Saga:** the framed hand collection from 'Treasure hunt', story script, **GUARDIANS OF ANCORA** multimedia story downloads

☐ **Guardians' guidelines:** verse cards, time chart, timer, compass or free mobile phone app

☐ **Victuals:** drinks and snacks

☐ **Treasure map:** Bibles, *Guardian's Journals* or *Guardian's Stories*, pens, pencils, paper

☐ **Orison:** inflated balloons, stickers, plain sticky labels, string, art materials

☐ **Construction:** materials for your chosen craft option(s)

☐ **Games:** equipment for your chosen game option(s)

☐ **Treasure Chest:** for jokes, messages, questions and pictures

☐ **Drama:** script from page 91, costumes and props

☐ **Keeper's questions:** quiz questions

☐ **Benison:** compass or free mobile phone app

THE THIRD QUEST

COMPANY DUTIES
🕐 10 MINUTES

Remind the children about the Treasure Chest so they can add any items they have brought or write and draw something now.

Chat about the previous holiday club Quest and respond to comments and questions. Have any Guardians been using their 'special Guardian skill' in the club or elsewhere? Give some hints about today's Quest, to raise the children's expectations. You could practise the *Learn and remember* verse together, too.

In any time remaining, continue decorating your Company space, making it unique to your group of children.

GUARDIANS ASSEMBLE
🕐 45 MINUTES ALL TOGETHER

Once all the children are settled in the Hall of Memory, the Keeper of the Keys and Kal re-introduce themselves and then re-introduce Fabula and the Shiner (if you are featuring them).

Kal is carrying a strange object: a bunch of wires with random pieces of old computer spares attached – and he's drying himself with a huge towel. The Keeper welcomes all the Guardians and says how extra-pleased she is to see them all today: today's Quest is not an easy one and Ancora needs their help. The Keeper wants to know what Kal is up to.

Kal enthuses about being responsible for all the waterways of the city including the great aquavators, which move boats around the different levels of the city. He is an engineering genius and has made many improvements to the ancient waterways and aquavators during his time as the city's Aquaneer. He's got a bit of a problem today with a broken nanodefragmentometer (!) but he assures everyone that there is no need to worry: he'll be able to fix it... unless any of the Guardians have got a spare one, anywhere?

 **ANCORA HERALD**
The Shiner performs this script:

Honest Guardians don't despair –
Here's the news so, with some care
Heed the words that I will utter –
Or I'll spread your face with butter!

He produces a pack of butter from his robes, then gives it to the Keeper. As he reads the headlines, he shouts the words in capitals, as if he were a newspaper vendor on the street.

NEW STORY UNLOCKED BY GUARDIANS!

Yesterday, Guardians discovered a box of shoes, which helped us all discover the story of the Roman officer's servant. We found out more about the power of faith in Jesus. My favourite rules for living are: 'Never leave the house without a lantern full of firebugs', 'Always say thank you when someone gives you something' and 'Never eat anything from the fridge that's covered with more than 5 cm of mould'.

ANCORA'S GOT TALENT WINNER LOSES HER TALENT

The winner of this year's *Ancora's Got Talent* has lost her talent. Mrs Philomena Cornflake, who works in the market, won the contest with her dancing firebugs. However, early yesterday morning, when she was still half asleep, she used her firebug dance troop to light the lanterns in the market. 'I'm devastated,' she says. 'They're so happy in the lanterns that they won't come back and dance!'

SUCCESS FOR GUARDIANS!

The Guildmaster wants to congratulate [insert Company name here] **and** [insert another Company name here] **for their efforts at the club yesterday. They** [talk about what both companies did well]**. However, as I was wandering round yesterday, I saw some great stuff, so well done everyone!**

The Keeper and Kal assume that he will keep on talking, but today he has finished and acts surprised that they haven't got on with telling everyone about today's Quest, especially as they said it wasn't going to be an easy one: there's no time to waste!

 **TREASURE HUNT**
Before the session, prepare a set of clues (in envelopes or small packages) that will lead Kal and a small team of Guardians around the venue to, eventually, find buried treasure. Clues can be words, signs or objects. These can be as simple or elaborate as you choose and much will depend on the size of your meeting space and

the number of children attending. You will want the hunt to be fast-paced and exciting as most of the children will be observing rather than taking part, so don't be too obscure with the clues. Plan the route so Kal and his Guardian-team will have to crisscross the space and move around a lot. Aim for about ten clues and have the last clue take the Guardians to a hidden treasure, which is a very important-looking framed collection of handprints (make one from cardboard and spray-painted pasta shapes for the frame, and paint your own hands(!) for the prints) buried beneath a pile of scraps and general junk, tucked away in an unused corner of the room.

Kal asks for a few volunteer Guardians to help him today. Meanwhile, the Keeper has found a parcel or envelope. When she opens it, she is puzzled by what she finds inside. Kal points out that it must be the first clue for the treasure.

As always, Kal makes sure the Guardians have their equipment with them, and reminds them to keep together.

The Keeper reads the first clue and the treasure hunt is off! Each time they find a clue, someone should read it out. Involve the whole club in working out where the next clue might be, before setting off for the next location. The Firebugs could add to the atmosphere with music, silent-movie style!

When the hidden handprint collection is discovered, Kal gasps: this is a very precious story-treasure. Kal and his Guardian assistants need to guard it carefully as they make their way back to the Keeper. Kal makes the most of how difficult and dangerous it was and thinks it is obvious that the handprints are valuable: surely the Keeper doesn't need to worry? But the Keeper always does things the right way: Kal argues with her (a little) but she takes it calmly to her workstation to check.

GUARDIANS SINGING
Reintroduce the Firebugs and use mostly songs that you have already done with the children, perhaps including another new one, especially if some of the children could help the others to learn it. You could finish with the **GUARDIANS OF ANCORA** theme song, and include any actions you might have come up with!

STORY OF THE SAGA

Fabula will now be a familiar character to most of the children and they will know that she enjoys having newly-found stories of the Saga to tell. Today she is much happier because so many Guardians have come to the aid of Ancora and they have been so successful in finding lost stories. Fabula thanks them for joining the Guild and explains a little about her 'life' in Ancora. As the chief storyteller of the city, she makes sure that the stories of the Saga are always being told.

The Keeper brings today's story-treasure (the handprints, found during **Treasure hunt**) forward and presents it to Fabula, who treats it as something very precious. She thanks the Guardians again for finding another item and restoring it to the Keeper of the Keys.

Storytelling options

Each day, there are three options suggested for telling the Bible story: you can use the same approach each time, mix and match how you tell the story, or combine two or more approaches. Choose which will be most helpful for your team, your children and the style of your club.

I Fabula or another storyteller tells the story based on Luke 8:40–56 using their own words and personal storytelling style, if possible. You can use the section headings and ideas from the scripted version (see option III) as memory joggers and to vary your story presentation each time, if you wish.

II Introduce today's video storytelling episode available to download from the **GUARDIANS OF ANCORA** multimedia downloads area. (If you are telling the story and using the video, tell the story first, then show the video so the children already have the outline of the events before seeing the episode.)

III Or the storyteller may prefer to follow the fully scripted retold Bible story for Quest 3 on page 77.

GUARDIANS' GUIDELINES

'Jesus said: Love the Lord your God with all your heart, soul and mind.'
Matthew 22:37

As on previous days, invite a number of children to take the daily *Learn and remember* challenge: you will need 14 children.

Give out the cards, face down and, with a three, two, one countdown, start the timer. See how long it takes for the children to line up in verse order. (The Firebugs could play an urgent rhythm to speed them along.) Involve everyone in encouraging them, making suggestions, cheering and so on. Stop the timer, announce the result and record it on the chart, commenting on how it compares with previous tallies.

Ask whether anyone thinks they know the verse by heart. Say that you are about to find out! One of the skills of a Guardian is to find their way around: use a compass or a phone app to find out which way is north. All stand up and face that direction: say the *Learn and remember* verse together, without looking at the words if possible.

Turn to the south and repeat.

Turn east and say the verse; turn west and say the verse one more time.

Invite the members of one Company to come forward and lead the actions as you all sing the *Learn and remember* verse song a couple of times.

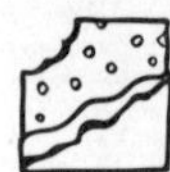

GUARDIANS' GOLD

Jairus thought that his daughter was dead, the woman thought she would be unwell forever, but they put their faith in Jesus and he intervened. You may not have an Elder Guardian who has experienced a physical healing, but you are likely to be able to find someone who has experienced God's intervention at some point in their lives. If you would prefer you could ask an Elder Guardian to speak about a time when Jesus has said or done something both unexpected and good. Interview an Elder Guardian about a time when Jesus has surprised them, in a good way. Was it easy for them to put their faith in Jesus? How were they able to tell that it was really God that intervened? How did this experience make them feel? What is the 'treasure' in their relationship with Jesus?

UNLOCK THE TREASURE

⏱ 45 MINUTES IN SMALL GROUPS

VICTUALS

Make sure the children are comfortable in their Companies, as they settle for their refreshments. Younger children can take longer over this, so you may want to begin talking about the story as they drink their drinks.

TREASURE MAP: BIBLE DISCOVERY

Welcome everyone back to your Company and use your motto or password to confirm your group identity. Chat about what you have been doing in the club so far. Ask whether the children enjoyed the treasure hunt. What did they think of the Bible story? Are there any questions they are keen to ask straight away or comments they are bursting to make?

With older children (8 to 11s)

Ask the children to think about a task they have had to complete that required a lot of attention to detail (eg a craft activity, a jigsaw puzzle, a hidden object computer game/app). Encourage them to say whether they found this easy or difficult. Why? It might be that some of the children in your group have a special Guardian skill that pertains to this. Have some ideas of your own to share too.

Today's **Story of the Saga** tells of two more miraculous healings. Say that they both teach us important things about what Jesus is like and what he wants those who follow him to be like. These miracles show us that Jesus really cares about the details of our lives. He knows everything that is happening to us and wants to help us.

Pause to think about what a 'miracle' is. See if you can get the children to come up with a definition as a group that you can all agree on and then invite them to write it on page 24 of *Guardian's Journal* or on paper.

Remind the children that, as Jesus travelled around, more and more people heard about the amazing things he had been doing. Challenge them to remember what happened to the Roman officer's servant yesterday. Invite them to share any other amazing things that they know Jesus did.

Read today's story, from *Guardian's Journal* page 22 or Luke 8:40–48. Ask the children: How do you think the woman felt when Jesus noticed she had touched his cloak? Why do you think

Jesus asked who had 'touched him'? Did he already know who it was?

Turn to page 23 or find Luke 8:49–56 and read what happens next. This may not be a surprise, if they have been listening to the **Story of the Saga**, but ask what the children think about it. Go through all the verses again and encourage the children to say which parts of the story they like the best, and why. Ask whether they notice anything similar in these stories to yesterday's story about the Roman officer's servant.

If you are using *Guardian's Journal*, spend time completing the wordsearch on page 21 and decode the messages on page 26.

Encourage the children to think about how the people in both stories came to Jesus for help. Say that one of the reasons Christians pray is to ask Jesus for help. Invite the children to use a sheet of paper or *Guardian's Journal* page 25 to write or draw their prayers. Encourage them to tell God what they are thinking, what they would like him to help with or what they want to thank him for – anything they like! Suggest the children could look at this paper/page another day and see how God has answered their prayers.

You may find that this topic brings up questions about why God doesn't always heal people. The children may have stories of when they have prayed for someone to be made well and they have remained unwell. Your church/organisation will likely have a well thought through answer to this question, which you should be prepared to use if necessary. Alternatively, you may like to refer to *So, Why God?* – a helpful resource published by Scripture Union to help you answer questions such as these (SU 978 1 84427 222 8).

In the face of such difficult questions it is helpful to remind children that no matter what our situation Jesus cares deeply for us and loves us very much. His desire is always to do what is best for us and he wants us to know that he is always with us even when things are hard and we don't understand what is happening.

With younger children (5 to 8s)

Ask if the children can remember who met Jesus in the **Story of the Saga** today.

Read the shortened version from *Guardian's Stories* pages 14 and 15 together; or read a shortened version of Luke 8:40–56 aloud to the children (prepare this beforehand as the verses are complex for younger children to follow).

Encourage the children to share their first impressions and reactions. Did they expect Jesus to heal these people? Are they surprised that Jesus didn't seem to know who had touched his coat? Can they imagine how Jairus and his wife might have felt when their little girl was dead, but then Jesus brought her back to life?

Remind the children that Jesus wants people who follow him and believe in him to try to live like he did. This means that he wants them to care for others and help where they can. Try to explain to the children that Christians do these things for Jesus because they love him, not just because they follow a set of rules. As a whole group come up with some practical ideas to help the children express care to those around them at home or school or in their community. Write these ideas down or draw pictures to represent them on page 16 of *Guardian's Stories* or on a sheet of paper.

Invite the children to say whether they think Jesus cared for the people in today's story. Ask if they understand that he cares for them too.

Say that, in the next Quest, they will be hearing about something else amazing that Jesus did, and about a group of people who did something quite extraordinary to help their friend see Jesus. Choose whether to tell the children that the next Quest is about a man who was lowered through a hole in a roof – or whether to leave them wondering about what might happen!

With all ages

Adapt these questions to suit your group, sharing your own feelings, opinions and experiences as appropriate (some are also in *Guardian's Journal* but are open-ended, with no right or wrong answer, so can be answered at any age):

- What have you discovered that you didn't know before?
- Has this story reminded you of anything you already knew?
- What do you want to think about some more?
- How are the characters in this story like you or someone you know?
- What is Jesus like in this story? Can you think of three words to describe him?
- How much do you think Jesus cares for you?o
- How can you care for and help other people?

USING THE **GUARDIANS ⊕F ANC⊕RA** APP WITH THIS QUEST

If you have access to a tablet and are able to download the **GUARDIANS ⊕F ANC⊕RA** app there are several ways you could use this to enhance today's quest.

- ⊕ If you are able to connect your tablet to a projector, you could play through relevant parts of 'Jesus and Jairus' as a way of introducing the story to the children.
- ⊕ If you have enough tablets to have one per company you could encourage children to take it turns playing through 'Jesus and Jairus' at appropriate points in your programme. You might like to set a time limit to make sure everyone gets a turn.

If you have enough tablets for one company to have one each, you could incorporate time during construction or games for companies to rotate and play through 'Jesus and Jairus' in a dedicated 'tablet zone' under supervision. You could suggest the following to the children:

- ⊕ Hot news! Jesus is arriving in town, by boat. Get yourself down to the lake to find him.
- ⊕ There's sad news about a girl who is poorly. Go with Jesus and see what he will do.
- ⊕ Find your way past the crowds – but don't miss exciting things along the way!

If you don't have access to a tablet, and aren't able to download the **GUARDIANS ⊕F ANC⊕RA** app yourself, don't worry, there are still plenty of exciting ways to engage with **GUARDIANS ⊕F ANC⊕RA**. You can start by visiting www.guardiansofancora.com to find out more!

Remember to encourage the children who attend your group to download the app for themselves if they have access to a tablet at home.

ORISON

Summarise what you've been discovering in Treasure map (or encourage one of the children to recap). Ask what the children think about it. What sticks in their memory? What do they want to say to God?

Explain that they are going to use the balloons as visual expressions of their prayers. Invite the children to decorate the balloons with ready-made stickers, or write and draw messages, pictures and symbols on plain labels and stick these on the balloons.

When the balloons are complete, tie them together with string and hang the bunch where the children can see it, perhaps as an extra item in your Company area; or the whole club could combine to make a massive prayer-balloon collection.

Take a moment to look at the balloons and remember the prayer messages on them. Suggest that the children could do that, every time they notice the balloons.

CONSTRUCTION

Choose a construction activity from the **Treasure Store** pages 80 to 83. There are craft ideas based on the **GUARDIANS OF ANCORA** theme and on the Bible teaching. Today's Bible construction is 'Handprint paining' on page 80.

For extra craft ideas, see *Ultimate Craft* (SU 978 1 84427 364 5).

GAMES

Help the Guardians shape up by choosing suitable games from pages 84 to 86. There are extra themed games at the **GUARDIANS OF ANCORA** multimedia downloads area. For even more games ideas see *Ultimate Games* (SU 978 1 84427 365 2).

GUARDIANS' GATHERING
🕐 25 MINUTES ALL TOGETHER

TREASURE CHEST

Welcome everyone back together again by playing the **GUARDIANS OF ANCORA** theme song. Read out some of the jokes, messages, questions and pictures in the Treasure Chest today. Thank all the contributing Guardians and encourage them to bring more jokes, messages, pictures and questions to post in Treasure Chest tomorrow.

COMPANY SHOWCASE

Choose a Company and invite the Elder Guardian and two or three of the children to the front to show everyone something they have been doing. It might be an item they have made to decorate their space, an emblem or flag they have devised or a motto to say. Admire what they have shown and thank them for being enthusiastic Guardians.

THE SEARCH FOR THE GOLDEN SHIELD

Recap on yesterday's adventure, for anyone who missed the session. Introduce the day's episode from *The Search for the Golden Shield*. Swift dreams of finding the shield and building a monument to it so that people can remember its story. But Swift's ambitions cause problems between her and her friend Dash. Is there any hope for Swift – and the quest?

KEEPER'S QUESTIONS

Divide the children into evenly-matched teams and devise a quiz that relates to all that has happened during your **GUARDIANS OF ANCORA** holiday club so far. This can include funny events that happened unique to your club (show images on the screen if you have been making a photographic record), as well as facts from the stories and the *Learn and remember* verse.

Alternatively you can use the quiz from page 102 or from the **GUARDIANS OF ANCORA** multimedia downloads area based on the Bible story from Quest 3.

BENISON

If you used the compass to find directions during 'Guardian's guidelines', see if the Guardians can remember which way is north; or ask for volunteers to help you use a compass or a phone app now. Remind the children that in today's Bible story crowds had gathered to hear from Jesus. People were beginning to respect Jesus, they were intrigued by him, his disciples followed his every lead. Jesus was getting a bit of a reputation as a man who could do amazing things, a man who could heal people.

Focus this time together as an opportunity to pray for those who are unwell – asking God to bring healing, strength, peace and restoration. Stand with everyone facing in the same direction and pray for God to bring healing to people who you or the

children know who are unwell in some way. Turn through 90° and ask God to bring strength to these people. Turn again and pray that he would bring peace. Turn another 90° and pray for God to bring restoration. Return to your starting position and use David's words from 2 Samuel 7:22 as a praise shout:

Lord All-Powerful!
You are greater than all others.
No one is like you
And you alone are God!

REVIVE!

The Firebugs lead the children in a couple of lively songs.

Round off **Guardians' gathering** by asking two children to say in one sentence what one thing they will share when they get home. Children are used to doing this in school. Elder Guardians can ask a similar question when the children are back in their Companies.

The Shiner reminds everyone about the collection procedure, and assures them that he is looking forward to seeing them the next day. Where will the story-treasure be hidden and what will it be? What story will be unlocked by the story-treasure? What news will there be from Ancora? Sing the **GUARDIANS OF ANCORA** theme song one more time and then send the children back to their Companies.

SIGNING OFF
🕐 10 MINUTES

Chat about what 'special Guardian skills' would be useful for the **GUARDIANS IN ANCORA**. The children all have their own skills, but what skill should the Keeper of the Keys have? What about Kal, Fabula and the Shiner? In the drama, Swift certainly needs seeker skills: what would the children suggest?

RESTORATION: CLEARING UP AND A QUICK DEBRIEF

Once the children have gone, tidy up and do any necessary preparation for the following day. As many as possible in the team should meet to debrief on how the session has gone, identify any hitches that could be put right or any children who have been unhappy, report back on how the session in each Company has been and spend time praying together.

Remember to acknowledge and affirm team members' contributions to the session. If possible, share a meal together (although you may only wish to do that on the last day).

QUEST IV
JESUS HEALS A MAN WHO CAME THROUGH A ROOF!

KEY PASSAGE
Luke 5:17-26

KEY STORYLINES

⊕ The Guardians unwrap a selection of random objects, the last of which is a mat, leading them to the story of Jesus healing a man who comes to him through a hole in a roof!

⊕ A paralysed man is brought to Jesus, but because there is no space for the men carrying him to get through the crowds they climb onto the roof of the building where Jesus is teaching and lower the man through the ceiling.

⊕ On seeing the faith of these men, Jesus heals the paralysed man.

KEY AIMS

⊕ To understand that God has the power to heal and restore.

⊕ To identify that in each of the healing miracles explored so far Jesus comments on the faith of the people involved.

⊕ To realise that part of being healed and restored is being forgiven, and that Jesus has the power to forgive our sins.

⊕ To grasp what it means to put faith in Jesus day to day.

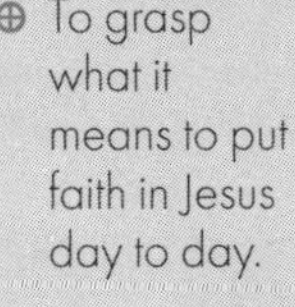

GUARDIANS BACKGROUND

NO CHURCH BACKGROUND

Children with little or no experience of church are likely to be confused by the Pharisees. They were law-abiding citizens, and kept God's rules, so why doesn't Jesus seem to like them? Try to explain to the children that the Pharisees were Jewish people who had studied their Scriptures in great depth to help them follow God's will. But they had forgotten to love God first and foremost and had started to follow the rules just because they were rules!

Some children may also find the idea of Jesus healing people difficult to comprehend, especially when they learn that Christians believe Jesus still heals today. Remind the children that Jesus heals by letting God the Father work through him, and so God can still use people to do that today. Remember to take time to explain words like 'sin' and 'forgiveness' – sin doesn't have to mean being wicked, it means missing perfection!

CHURCH CHILDREN

This group are likely to take forgiveness for granted, as it is a key element of our beliefs. They may have interesting ideas about sin, though – that there is a hierarchy of sin (get them to think about why God sees every sin as equally sinful) or that because God is gracious it doesn't matter if we keep on sinning. Encourage them to explore why dealing with sin may be a higher priority for God than physical healing – we can live with imperfect bodies, but our relationship with God is much more of a challenge if we do not deal with our sin.

WITH OTHER FAITHS

Judaism now suggests that God alone can forgive sins against him, but those who have sinned against other people must first seek their forgiveness; without repentance (which the sick man here does not show) there can be no forgiveness. Yet it is also a religious duty to forgive when asked. This is also true in Islam, where Allah is viewed as a gracious, compassionate God, and his people must follow his example. However, Allah alone can forgive sins against him. Similarly, the eastern faiths such as Sikhism, Hinduism and Buddhism place great emphasis on forgiveness – chiefly to liberate the one sinned against. Within Jainism, the most common form of greeting is an asking pardon for unwitting hurt or offence. Some world faiths still see sickness as a sign of God's disfavour. In animistic religions, sickness may be the result of a curse, which may be broken by forgiveness.

WITH ADDITIONAL NEEDS

Every child with additional needs will be very different, and your approach with each will need to vary. For some of the children, lying down on a mat while they think about Jesus forgiving the man lowered through the roof would be a good multi-sensory teaching tool. Occasionally, children with additional needs will find waiting and queuing difficult, so maybe looking at the story from the point of view of the friends not wanting to wait to go through the door could be helpful. For others, simply looking at the thankfulness aspect of the teaching would be more appropriate. Sometimes children with additional needs don't have many friends, so a little sensitivity may be needed.

ELDER **GUARDIANS** GATHER

Feeling weary, after energetic Quests? Or more energised than ever? However you are feeling, take a few minutes to pray, share and prepare together to give you the strength, kindness and energy for another Quest.

SPIRITUAL PREPARATION

Read Luke 5:17–26 together.

Ask members of the group to share their thoughts on the passage.

For some children (and adults too!) the healing miracles can sometimes be problematic. As a group, discuss the following questions and consider how you might respond if asked a similar question by a child at your club:
⊕ When we pray for people today and ask Jesus to restore them, why are they not healed?
⊕ How do we know God really cares for us?
⊕ Why do bad things happen to good people?

As you consider this story, encourage people to notice the persistence of those who brought the ill man to Jesus. Remind everyone that sometimes our own relationships with Jesus require persistence and determination, too, no matter how long or short a time we've known him. Spend a few minutes discussing the following questions together:
⊕ Why does Jesus say 'My friend, your sins are forgiven' rather than immediately proclaiming healing?
⊕ How you might have felt if you were the man?
⊕ Why do the Pharisees react in the way they do? Who do they think Jesus is?

Spend some time in prayer thanking God for his healing power and grace. Thank God that Jesus is alive today and working in the world through the Holy Spirit.

Ask church leaders and those who pray regularly to pray for the club today throughout the day. You might like to suggest that they pray for God's protection and the ability for everyone to understand God's power, authority, compassion and mercy.

Encourage everyone to pray for each other throughout the session. If you have time, spend a few moments praying for one another before you continue.

PRACTICAL PREPARATION

Talk through your programme together. Remind everyone of the key learning aims and who is doing what, ensuring that everyone knows their part in the day and has everything they need.

Set up the different areas of the club and make sure that everything is in place in plenty of time, so you are ready as the first children come from the registration area.

Listen to any last-minute information or instructions from the Guildmaster, Keeper or Kal, or from the drama, music or refreshment team. By now the children are likely to be joining in willingly and noisily: remind the team to keep an eye out for those who may be keeping on the fringe and those who may be getting over excited.

WHAT-YOU-NEED CHECKLIST

☐ **Registration:** registration forms, badges, labels, pens, team lists, paper firebugs

☐ **Ancora Herald:** today's news, 'Marmite' pie

☐ **Treasure hunt:** a selection of random objects including some sort of mat all wrapped into a giant Pass the Parcel, bags for litter, music to stop and start

☐ **Music:** Firebugs band or backing tracks

☐ **Story of the Saga:** the mat found in 'Treasure hunt', story script, **GUARDIANS OF ANCORA** multimedia story downloads

☐ **Guardians' guidelines:** verse cards, time chart, timer

☐ **Victuals:** drinks and snacks

☐ **Treasure map:** Bibles, *Guardian's Journals* or *Guardian's Stories*, pens, pencils, paper

☐ **Orison:** magnetic words or letters; magnetic surfaces to put them on; or words and letters on pieces of card

☐ **Construction:** materials for your chosen craft option(s)

☐ **Games:** equipment for your chosen game option(s)

☐ **Treasure Chest:** for jokes, messages, questions and pictures

☐ **Drama:** script from page 92, costumes and props

☐ **Keeper's questions:** quiz questions

THE FOURTH QUEST

COMPANY DUTIES
🕐 10 MINUTES

Remind the children about the **Treasure Chest** so they can add any items they have brought or write and draw something now.

Chat about the previous holiday club Quests and respond to comments and questions. Have any Guardians been using their 'special Guardian skill' in the club or elsewhere? Give some hints about today's Quest, to raise the children's expectations. You could practise the *Learn and remember* verse together, too.

In any time remaining before **Guardians assemble**, continue decorating your Company space, making it unique to your group of children.

GUARDIANS ASSEMBLE
🕐 45 MINUTES ALL TOGETHER

Once all the children are settled in the Hall of Memory, the Keeper of the Keys and Kal re-introduce themselves and then re-introduce Fabula and the Shiner (if you are featuring them). The upfront presenters set an enthusiastic and adventurous tone to the programme and encourage the Guardians to be part of the daily life of Ancora.

They chat together and to the children about some of the best bits of the holiday club so far, mentioning and reliving a range of memorable moments. They ask the children what they have been enjoying most, suggest three 'moments' and get everyone to clap for each, depending on how much they liked it. Declare a 'winning moment'.

 **ANCORA HERALD**
The Shiner performs this script:

Listen friends to what I say,
To the headlines from today.
Look at me with a keen eye
Or you'll face this Marmite pie!

He produces a pie filled with dark brown goo from his robes, then gives it to the Keeper. As he reads the headlines, he shouts the words in capitals, as if he were a newspaper vendor on the street.

SPREADING BUTTER ON PEOPLE'S FACES DECLARED ILLEGAL!

Yesterday, I threatened to spread butter on your face if you didn't listen to my news. However, face buttering has been outlawed by the Guildmaster. In a statement, he said, 'Why is the Shiner wasting butter? It shouldn't be spread on people's faces, it should be spread on my toast!' Controversial!

GUARDIANS REACH NEW HEIGHTS

Special commendations today go to *[insert Company name here]* and *[insert another Company name here]*. They *[talk about what both companies did well]*. My storytelling colleague, Fabula, tells me that all the teams of Guardians did a great job yesterday!

NEW STORIES FOUND FOR THE SPIRE

Yesterday, Guardians uncovered a new story-treasure – a beautiful collection of handprints. The prints helped us find out more about Jesus and some of the amazing things he did. I have decided to get some new gloves made to help me remember the story – look out for those tomorrow!

The Keeper and Kal say that now they will tell everyone about today's Quest.

 **TREASURE HUNT**
Before the session, wrap each of your random items into a layer of your pass the parcel. Depending upon the size of your group you may choose to include layers with no object, or you may want objects in every layer. Decide if you want to include sweets or treats in each layer too, and if so be sure to check for allergies and intolerances in your groups. By the time you've finished your parcel it should be quite large!

The Keeper explains that she has been given this enormous parcel but she hasn't got time to unwrap it all herself: can the children help? Perhaps there is a story-treasure inside! Play live or recorded music, while the children pass the parcel around and then stop: allow time for whoever is holding the parcel to peel off one layer.

After all the layers have been removed, the Guardians will have uncovered a collection of rather odd objects, including a mat. Kal should ask the children who uncovered the objects to come to the front and present their items to the Keeper, who holds each one up high for everyone to see, with

plenty of cheering. As more and more objects are held up, Kal can get more lively and excited while the Keeper becomes absorbed in having so many potential story-treasures at the same time.

After all the items have been shown the Keeper gathers up all the pieces and carries them to her workstation. She starts checking the items to see if any are genuine story-treasures and the key to one of the stories of the Saga, while Kal introduces the Firebug band...

 **GUARDIANS SINGING**
Reintroduce the Firebugs and sing the **GUARDIANS OF ANCORA** theme song, along with any actions. Sing a song that you have already sung at **GUARDIANS OF ANCORA** and introduce a new one today, related to today's theme.

STORY OF THE SAGA
Fabula comes on stage alone and is impatient to know whether the Guardians have been successful today. She asks what they have been doing: did they go on a treasure hunt? Were they successful? What did they find? And *where is it*? Fabula hurries off to find the Keeper. Meanwhile, the Keeper enters from the other direction, bringing only the mat. If your building allows, have Fabula and the Keeper look for each other and keep 'just missing' each other, with the children adding plenty of encouragement (pantomime style).

When they eventually meet up, the Keeper presents today's story-treasure to Fabula (the mat found in 'Treasure hunt'), and tells her that among all the objects the children found only one, this old mat is a genuine story-treasure. Fabula instantly calms down and holds the item, in obvious wonder. These are stories she loves to tell and she thanks the Guardians for making it possible.

Storytelling options
Each day, there are three options suggested for telling the Bible story: you can use the same approach each time, mix and match how you tell the story or combine two or more approaches. Choose which will be most helpful for your team, your children and the style of your club.

1 Fabula or another storyteller tells the story based on Luke 5:17–26 using their own words and personal

storytelling style, if possible. You can use the section headings and ideas from the scripted version (see option III) as memory joggers and to vary your story presentation each time, if you wish.

II Introduce today's video storytelling episode available to download from the **GUARDIANS ⊕F ANC⊕RA** multimedia downloads area. (If you are telling the story and using the video, tell the story first, then show the video so the children already have the outline of the events before seeing the episode.)

III Or the storyteller may prefer to follow the fully scripted retold Bible story for Quest 4 on page 78.

GUARDIANS' GUIDELINES

'Jesus said: Love the Lord your God with all your heart, soul and mind.'
Matthew 22:37

By now the children will be familiar with the verse – and with the daily 'time how long it takes to put the words in order' challenge. As before, hand out the words at random and time how long it takes for the children to arrange themselves so that the verse reads correctly. Record the time: are you getting faster or about the same?

Say the words together and then ask if anyone can think of something they could do that would help them love the Lord more. One thing that we can do to show that we love the Lord is to tell stories about Jesus to others: remind the Guardians that they have been hearing some of those stories already (in the stories of the Saga) and will be finding out more today.

Before that, suggest you have a good time and have some fun with the good news by doing a Mexican wave. Form a circle around the room (it can be several people deep). Go clockwise around the circle. Choose someone to start. They stand up, raise their arms in the air, lower their arms and sit down. Immediately, the person on their left does the same, and so the action is passed around the circle. Practise a few times to get the wave going: ideally you need about 25 people for an effective wave, but it's still fun to try if you have fewer.

Now add the *Learn and remember* verse, so the words flow around the circle, just as the wave does.

Sing the *Learn and remember* verse song, first with the music, then with

no accompaniment. Sing a third time, loudly with the music again and with enthusiastic actions.

GUARDIANS' GOLD

Interview a leader by first asking them to briefly say what it means to them that Jesus loves them. How do they know he does? How do they feel about having their sins forgiven through what Jesus did? Encourage them to briefly say how they have come to be a follower of Jesus and to give a recent example of what it means to have Jesus as their friend. What is the 'treasure' in their relationship with Jesus?

UNLOCK THE TREASURE
⏱ 45 MINUTES IN SMALL GROUPS

VICTUALS

Make sure the children are comfortable in their Companies, as they settle for their refreshments. Younger children can take longer over this, so you may want to begin talking about the story as they drink their drinks.

TREASURE MAP: BIBLE DISCOVERY

With older children (8 to 11s)
Ask the children if they have ever had to wait in a queue for something. How did it feel? How long did they have to wait? Did they get what they wanted when they eventually got to the front of the queue?

Challenge them to remember what Jesus did in yesterday's story. As you give out *Guardian's Journals* or Bibles, say that you're going to be finding out about another story in which Jesus performed another miracle. (See if the children can remember your definition of 'miracle' from Quest 3.)

Summarise the healing miracles from Jesus' ministry that you have explored so far in a few sentences.

Read Luke 5:17–26 from *Guardian's Journal* page 29 or from a Bible, and ask the children to look out for something rather odd that happened in today's story. Ask the children to imagine what the story scene must have looked like.

By now children will be expecting Jesus to perform yet another miraculous healing. Try to encourage them to realise that this is still an amazing event! Ask the children how they might have felt to see a man being lowered

through a roof on a mat. Why do they think the man's friends were so desperate to get him to Jesus? Why didn't they just stand in a queue outside the house and wait? Challenge them to remember what Jesus said to the man.

Invite the children to turn to *Guardian's Journal* page 32 (Luke 5:20 in the Bible) and notice the words of Jesus. Read the Bible verse again and invite the children to express their first thoughts on hearing what Jesus says. Doesn't it seem a bit odd that Jesus says this? Why doesn't he just say 'you are healed', or 'your faith is amazing' like he did in the stories from previous Quests? What do Jesus' words tell us about him?

Explain that Jesus is the Son of God the Father. The Father sent Jesus to earth to forgive sins and help us to rebuild our relationship with him. The man in today's story needed to be friends with God again and he couldn't do that unless his sins were forgiven. Depending upon the understanding of the children in your group you may want to take some time at this point to explore what sin is and how it separates us from God as well as how the work of Jesus on the cross restores this relationship. Explain to the children that Jesus will forgive their sins too if they ask him, because he loves them very much and that he wants to be their lifelong friend.

Encourage any child who wants to know more about following Jesus to talk with you or suggest who else they might like to talk with (remember to follow your church's safeguarding policy).

With younger children (5 to 8s)
Invite the children to think back to the previous Quest and the two women that were healed.

Ask who the **Story of the Saga** was about today. Who were the characters in the story? What happened at the beginning, middle and end? Encourage the children to remember some of the details of the story, and ask whether anything unexpected happened.

Complete *Guardian's Stories* page 19 or ask the children to draw four pictures of today's story: a big crowd of people outside a house; the unwell man on his mat; the man and his friends on the roof; the man standing up and looking well.

Turn to *Guardian's Stories* page 18 or find Luke 5:25 in a Bible and read the verse. Ask the children why the man was praising God. Encourage them to think of anything they want to say thank you to God for. Start to collect words and phrases that express how the children think and feel about God.

Invite the children to complete *Guardian's Stories* page 20 with words and pictures that show what they want to thank God for; or add words and more pictures to the story scenes made earlier.

With all ages

Adapt these questions to suit your group, sharing your own feelings, opinions and experiences as appropriate (some are also in *Guardian's Journal* but are open-ended, with no right or wrong answer, so can be answered at any age):

⊕ What have you discovered that you didn't know before?
⊕ Has this story (or these stories) reminded you of anything you already knew?
⊕ What do you want to think about some more?
⊕ Is it what you thought would happen? Why – or why not? What *did* you expect?
⊕ What would it have been like to be there?
⊕ How does it make you feel that Jesus wants to be your friend?
⊕ What have you learnt about God from today's story/stories?

Encourage any child who wants to know more about following Jesus to talk with you or suggest who else they might like to talk with (remember to follow your church's safeguarding policy).

ORISON

Explain that you are going to use magnetic words and letters to pray today.

With children in pairs or threes, ask one pair to write a prayer for the rest of the group to say to God. It could be a single word as a prompt for praying aloud; or a whole statement or sentence. (Be ready, discreetly, to monitor their ideas and help keep them God-focused.) Give them a few moments to construct the phrase and then all say the words aloud together as a prayer. Repeat several times, so all the children have an opportunity to lead the prayer thoughts for you all. You may find they would like more than one turn, as their prayer ideas flow.

(You could take a digital photo of each prayer and print it up to add to your Company area tomorrow.)

CONSTRUCTION

Choose a construction activity from the Treasure Store pages 80 to 83. There are craft ideas based on the **GUARDIANS ⊕F ANC⊕RA** theme and on the Bible teaching. Today's Bible construction is 'Woven mat' on page 81.

For extra craft ideas, see *Ultimate Craft* (SU 978 1 84427 364 5).

GAMES

Help the Guardians shape up by choosing suitable games from pages 84 to 86. There are extra themed games at the **GUARDIANS ⊕F ANC⊕RA** multimedia downloads area. For even more games ideas see *Ultimate Games* (SU 978 1 84427 365 2).

GUARDIANS' GATHERING
🕐 25 MINUTES ALL TOGETHER

TREASURE CHEST

Welcome everyone back by playing the **GUARDIANS ⊕F ANC⊕RA** theme song. Read out a selection of the jokes, messages, pictures and comments in the Treasure Chest today. Thank all the Guardians for their post and encourage them to bring their jokes, messages, pictures and questions next time – there is only one day left of **GUARDIANS ⊕F ANC⊕RA**!

COMPANY SHOWCASE

Choose a Company and invite the Elder Guardian and two or three of the children to the front to show everyone something they have been doing. It might be an item they have made to decorate their space, an emblem or flag they have devised or a motto to say. Admire what they have shown and thank them for being enthusiastic Guardians.

THE SEARCH FOR THE GOLDEN SHIELD

See if the children can remember what has happened so far in *The Search for the Golden Shield*, and recap on yesterday's adventure, for anyone who missed the session.

Introduce the next episode of the drama. Today, Swift is in deep trouble, but she is rescued by an unlikely saviour! She realises what it really takes to be a Guardian and almost gives up – until a wise companion shows her that *now* she is truly ready to take the quest.

If you have access to a tablet and are able to download the **GUARDIANS ⊕F ANC⊕RA** app there are several ways you could use this to enhance today's quest.

⊕ If you are able to connect your tablet to a projector, you could play through relevant parts of 'Jesus forgives and heals' as a way of introducing the story to the children.
⊕ If you have enough tablets to have one per company you could encourage children to take it turns playing through 'Jesus forgives and heals' at appropriate points in your programme. You might like to set a time limit to make sure everyone gets a turn.

If you have enough tablets for one company to have one each, you could incorporate time during construction or games for companies to rotate and play through 'Jesus forgives and heals' in a dedicated 'tablet zone' under supervision. You could suggest the following to the children:

⊕ Something is going on in the town: find your way down there and see what's happening.
⊕ People everywhere! How will you get to see Jesus?
⊕ What about those poor-looking men? Is there any point in them trying to carry their friend to Jesus?

If you don't have access to a tablet, and aren't able to download the **GUARDIANS ⊕F ANC⊕RA** app yourself, don't worry, there are still plenty of exciting ways to engage with **GUARDIANS ⊕F ANC⊕RA**. You can start by visiting www.guardiansofancora.com to find out more!

Remember to encourage the children who attend your group to download the app for themselves if they have access to a tablet at home.

KEEPER'S QUESTIONS

Divide the children into evenly-matched teams and devise a quiz that relates to all that has happened during your **GUARDIANS OF ANCORA** holiday club so far. This can include funny events that happened unique to your club (show images on the screen if you have been making a photographic record), as well as facts from the stories and the *Learn and remember* verse.

Alternatively you can use the quiz from page 103 or from the **GUARDIANS OF ANCORA** multimedia downloads area based on the Bible story from Quest 4.

BENISON

Kal is eager to try using the pattern of a Mexican wave for your all-together prayer time today. (This will be quicker to organise if you also used the idea in 'Guardian's guidelines'.)

Form a circle around the room (it can be several people deep). Go clockwise around the circle. Choose someone to start. They stand up, raise their arms in the air, lower their arms and sit down. Immediately, the person on their left does the same, and so the action is passed around the circle. Practise a few times to get the wave going: ideally you need about 25 people for an effective wave but it's still fun to try, if you have fewer.

Now add words of praise and prayer, so the words flow around the circle, just as the wave does. Choose short phrases such as: Thank you, Jesus; Praise God for Jesus; Jesus is alive today. Encourage the children to contribute prayer-phrases to pass around on the 'wave'.

REVIVE!

The Firebugs lead the children in a couple of lively songs.

Round off **Guardians' gathering** by asking two children to say in one sentence what one thing they will share when they get home. Children are used to doing this in school. Elder Guardians can ask a similar question when the children are back in their Companies.

Fabula reminds everyone about the collection procedure, and assures them that she is looking forward to seeing them the next day. Where will the story-treasure be hidden and what will it be? What story will be unlocked? Will there be news from the Ancora Herald?

Sing the **GUARDIANS OF ANCORA** theme song one more time and then send the children back to their Companies.

SIGNING OFF
🕐 10 MINUTES IN SMALL GROUPS

If you have been using these few minutes to talk about Guardian skills, read the following list aloud and chat about whether and how each of these qualities would make a great Guardian: loving, happy, peaceful, patient, kind, good, faithful, gentle, self-controlled. (This is from Galatians 5:22,23a, if you wish to give the source of the list.)

RESTORATION: CLEARING UP AND A QUICK DEBRIEF

Once the children have gone, tidy up and do any necessary preparation for the following day. As many as possible in the team should meet to debrief on how the session has gone, identify any hitches that could be put right or any children who have been unhappy, report back on how children and leaders in each Company have settled and spend some time praying together.

Remember to acknowledge and affirm team members' contributions to the session. If possible, share a meal together (although you may only wish to do that on the last day).

QUEST V
JESUS FEEDS 5,000

KEY PASSAGES
John 6:1-15,25-35

KEY STORYLINES
⊕ The Guardians find tins of tuna and bread rolls, which reveal the story of Jesus feeding 5,000 people.
⊕ A crowd of people who have seen Jesus perform miracles and heal the sick are following him, eager to find out more about him.
⊕ Jesus takes two small fish and five loaves from a young boy and miraculously multiplies the food to feed the entire crowd, with twelve full baskets of leftovers.

KEY AIMS
⊕ To welcome each child to the club and to give them a memorable final day.
⊕ To discover that Jesus is able to use what we have to great effect when we allow him to do so.
⊕ To understand what Jesus means when he describes himself as 'the bread of life'.
⊕ To consider what it means to have a personal relationship with Jesus and to respond.

GUARDIANS BACKGROUND

NO CHURCH BACKGROUND
Depending upon their age and background some children may know a little about Judaism from school, they may even know that Jewish people celebrate the Passover meal. Try to find out what they already know (if anything!) and then fill in any gaps in their knowledge. Remind the children that every year Jews remember when God rescued them from slavery in Egypt and fed them for 40 years as they wandered in the desert getting to Israel.

When Jesus feeds the people in today's story miraculously some of them start to believe he might be the Messiah. Explain to the children what 'Messiah' means (anointed or chosen one) and tell them that the Jewish people had been waiting for their Messiah for a long time.

Understanding that Jesus is 'the bread of life' can be hard for children with no church background. Try to help them to understand his analogy – he is the 'bread' that will feed them spiritually.

CHURCH CHILDREN
The children probably know this story quite well, but like some of the crowd, they may well focus on how such a small amount of fish produced such a large quantity of leftovers (a basketful for each disciple or tribe of Israel). Although it is good to focus on God's generosity, and his willingness to use what we offer him, no matter how small it seems, the real lesson is about coming to know God so that we can have nourishment that gives us eternal life, not just full tummies. It may be rather faith-stretching to ask the children what they expect when they pray; Jesus was a man, but praying in faith he used a small packed lunch to feed 10,000 or more people. Do they expect miracles when they pray? Do they realise that faith, not good works, saves them?

WITH OTHER FAITHS
Despite what some formal theology says, members of every faith have expectations that God will answer prayer. Many have stories of God or gods performing miracles in response to prayer. Children with faith will be unlikely to doubt the ability for miracles to occur. Buddhism has no core belief in God or gods. There is a belief that the power of the mind can produce miracles, but these are no evidence of holiness and frowned upon unless serving another. Jewish children may well see the echoes of the provision of manna in the desert and may be more intrigued by the Judaic references in the text than other children. Encourage them to discuss their understanding and ask them what they feel about the fact that, after the miracle, some of the crowd speculated that Jesus might be the Messiah.

WITH ADDITIONAL NEEDS
'Bread of Life' is a difficult concept for some children to understand. If allergies permit, eating some bread and talking about how it helps our bodies to grow is a good start. Try not to use phrases such as 'Jesus is the bread…', because Jesus isn't a slice of bread! Instead, say he is like bread. In the same way that bread is good for us and helps us to grow healthily, following Jesus is good for us in many other ways. Discuss what those 'other ways' might be. The children with additional needs and disabilities may want to come to your midweek and Sunday groups. Make it clear on follow-up fliers that your children's work is accessible.

ELDER **GUARDIANS** GATHER

It's still important to meet together today. You will have settled into a club routine but, today, that routine will have an extra edge of urgency as it's the last time you meet in just this way. Celebrate as you meet, pray and prepare together.

SPIRITUAL PREPARATION

Read John 6:1–15,25–35 together.

Invite everyone to take some time to imagine the scene from the perspective of the different characters mentioned. Jesus takes a very small amount of food from a young boy and miraculously feeds over 5,000 people. Invite people to feed back on their reflections.

If it hasn't already been shared, point out that the disciples can't see a way around the situation they face until Jesus intervenes.

Spend some time praying together for God to intervene in situations in your own life or in the lives of those you know that seem impossible. Also pray by name for each child you deal with at club, that they might be willing to give Jesus what they have, knowing that he will do amazing things.

Split into small groups or pairs and pray in thanks for all the good things that have happened at your club, for relationships that have been built and for the truth that has been made known.

Finally, pray together about what will happen once the club has finished; for the children, for their families, for the team and their families and for the church or churches represented on the team. Pray that God will continue to bless you all, and to reveal himself more and more to those who have glimpsed who Jesus is.

PRACTICAL PREPARATION

Talk through your programme together. Remind everyone of the key learning aims and who is doing what, ensuring that everyone knows their part in the day and has everything they need.

Set up the different areas of the club and make sure that everything is in place in plenty of time, so you are ready as the first children come from the registration area.

Listen to any last-minute information or instructions from the Guildmaster, Keeper or Kal, or from the drama, music or refreshment team.

WHAT-YOU-NEED CHECKLIST

- [ ] **Registration:** registration forms, badges, labels, pens, team lists, paper firebugs
- [ ] **Guardians assemble:** fishing net, 'Roman' sandals, collection of handprints, a mat
- [ ] **Ancora Herald:** today's news, a dirty towel, a pair of heavily decorated gloves
- [ ] **Treasure hunt:** shopping bags (enough for one per company), random items of food, two tins of tuna and five bread rolls
- [ ] **Music:** Firebugs band or backing tracks
- [ ] **Story of the Saga:** two tins of tuna and five bread rolls (from 'Treasure hunt'), story script, **GUARDIANS OF ANCORA** multimedia story downloads
- [ ] **Guardians' guidelines:** verse cards, time chart, timer, small rewards for learning the verse
- [ ] **Victuals:** drinks and snacks
- [ ] **Treasure map:** Bibles, *Guardian's Journals* or *Guardian's Stories*, pens, pencils, paper, a Bible atlas or map
- [ ] **Orison:** sturdy candles and means to light them
- [ ] **Construction:** materials for your chosen craft option(s)
- [ ] **Games:** equipment for your chosen game option(s)
- [ ] **Treasure Chest:** for jokes, messages, questions and pictures
- [ ] **Drama:** script from page 93, costumes and props
- [ ] **Keeper's questions:** quiz questions

THE FIFTH **QUEST**

COMPANY DUTIES
🕐 10 MINUTES

Remind the children about the Treasure Chest so they can add any items they have brought, or write and draw something now.

Chat about the previous holiday club Quest and respond to comments and questions. Give some hints about today's Quest, to raise the children's expectations. You could practise the *Learn and remember* verse, together, too.

In any time remaining before **Guardians assemble**, continue decorating your Company space, making it unique to your group of children.

GUARDIANS ASSEMBLE
🕐 45 MINUTES ALL TOGETHER

Once all the children are settled in the Hall of Memory, the Keeper of the Keys and Kal re-introduce themselves and then re-introduce Fabula and the Shiner (if you are featuring them). The upfront presenters set an enthusiastic and adventurous tone to the programme and encourage the Guardians to be part of the 'daily life' of Ancora. As this is the last club-day of **GUARDIANS ⊕F ANC⊕RA**, show extra eagerness and urge the children to make the very best and most of this day's Quest.

The Keeper has four story-treasures about her person (fishing nets, 'Roman' sandals, a collection of handprints and a mat – all the objects used in the previous four Quests). She brings them out one by one, asking the children if they can remember the stories they represent and, most importantly, if they can remember what they learnt about Jesus from each story. As the Keeper is asking the children about the mat (from Quest 4), the Shiner arrives and tries to add the mat to his costume as an additional hat. The Keeper tells the Shiner he can't have the mat because it's an important story-treasure and a silly argument ensues. In the end, the Keeper leaves with all the story-treasures carefully stored about her person again and the Shiner looks sad, but then remembers his news.

ANCORA HERALD
The Shiner performs this script:

Hear ye, hear ye, it is the news!
So keep your hisses and your boos –
Or I'll drop upon your head
This manky towel from my dog's bed!

He produces a dirty towel from his robes and throws it to the Keeper (who should hold it at arm's length). As he reads the headlines, he shouts the words in capitals, as if he were a newspaper vendor on the street.

SHINER'S NEW GLOVES THE TALK OF THE FASHION WORLD

The Shiner – that's me! – has set Ancora talking about his new gloves. Compliments have been coming in thick and fast. 'They make a big statement!' said the Guildmaster. 'Words fail me,' said Fabula. 'They look like a pair of very tired guinea pigs who have fallen asleep on his hands,' said Swift.

SUCCESS FOR GUARDIANS

Guardians achieved great things yesterday! Special mention must go to *[insert Company name here]* and *[insert another Company name here]*. **They** *[talk about what both companies did well]*. **However, there were great things happening all over the place, so well done everyone!**

LAST DAY AT GUARDIANS OF ANCORA STARTS WITH A BANG

The last day at **GUARDIANS ⊕F ANC⊕RA** has started with a bang – I managed to blow up the kitchen while I was heating up some pop tarts! Yesterday, Guardians discovered the story of Jesus and a man who came through a hole in a roof, and today there is a new treasure to find.

The Keeper and Kal say that now they will tell everyone about today's quest.

TREASURE HUNT
Prior to your session hide several 'shopping bags' (enough for one per company) around your venue. Place random items of food in each bag, making sure that one bag contains only two tins of tuna and five bread rolls.

Invite one Company at a time (guided by their Elder Guardian) to hunt for a 'treasure bag'. When they find one, they bring it to the Keeper, who then unpacks the bag and looks confused at the selection of ingredients inside. The Keeper asks the Guardians what sort of meal they think could be made with these ingredients (the more ridiculous the better) and the Keeper looks disgusted. Then the children choose another Company who start searching. (Kal and other leaders will need to manage the changeover of Companies, to keep the game moving briskly while involving lots of children.) The 'treasure bags' can be found in any order.

When all the bags have been found, Kal is delighted to have found so much food but the Keeper is confused. She looks at the pile of food in front of her and then asks the children if they have any ideas about which find is the story-treasure (and why). She starts sorting through them: this can be quite an over-the-top performance, using tools such as a magnifying glass, her head torch, a set of scales, a microscope and so on. As she sets more and more items aside, Kal gets impatient to know if any of the items are real story-treasures until – ta-dah! – the Keeper holds up the two tins of tuna and five bread rolls. This is the story-treasure, she declares, and shows it to everyone. Kal is a little sceptical because it's just tuna and bread and, after all, there were all these other items found... But the Keeper is calm and certain: Kal will see, when she takes the tins and rolls to Fabula.

GUARDIANS SINGING
Reintroduce the Firebugs and sing the **GUARDIANS ⊕F ANC⊕RA** theme song, along with any actions. Sing some of the songs that you have already sung at **GUARDIANS ⊕F ANC⊕RA**, especially any that have become firm Guardian favourites over the course of your time together.

STORY OF THE SAGA
Fabula is in a happy mood because so many treasures are being found for the Hall of Memory. She thanks the Guardians for working so hard and tests them (lightheartedly) to see if they can remember what has been found on each day of the club, referring to the Keeper's 'parade' of story-treasures earlier on. She reminds the Guardians that there has been a treasure hunt

today and an object has been found. But what story could it reveal?

Fabula asks the Guardians to help call the Keeper of the Keys, who is sitting at the side of the room, busily shaking and sniffing the story-treasures discovered earlier (two tins of tuna and five bread' rolls, found in 'Treasure hunt'). The Keeper hears them, jumps up and hurries over to Fabula, to present the treasure. As always, Fabula handles it and admires it as something precious and wonderful. Are the Guardians ready for her to reveal the **Story of the Saga?**

Storytelling options

Each day, there are three options suggested for telling the Bible story: you can use the same approach each time, mix and match how you tell the story, or combine two or more approaches. Choose which will be most helpful for your team, your children and the style of your club.

I   Fabula or another storyteller tells the story based on John 6:1–15,25–35 using their own words and personal storytelling style, if possible. You can use the section headings and ideas from the scripted version (see option III) as memory joggers and to vary your story presentation each time, if you wish.

II   Introduce today's video storytelling episode available to download from the **GUARDIANS OF ANCORA** multimedia downloads area. (If you are telling the story and using the video, tell the story first, then show the video so the children already have the outline of the events before seeing the episode.)

III   Or the storyteller may prefer to follow the fully scripted retold Bible story for Quest 5 on pages 78 and 79.

GUARDIANS' GUIDELINES

'Jesus said: Love the Lord your God with all your heart, soul and mind.'
Matthew 22:37

By now many of the children will know this verse: ask for a few volunteers to come forward and say the words with no prompting. Then invite others to the front to take the daily *Learn and remember* challenge: for the verse from CEV, you will need 14 children.

Give out the cards, face down, and with a three, two, one countdown, start the timer. See how long it takes for the children to line up in verse order. (The Firebugs could play an urgent

rhythm to speed them along.) Involve everyone in encouraging them, making suggestions, cheering and so on. Stop the timer, announce the result and record it on the chart. Review the results and praise everyone for learning. (If you are using the verse in Service 2, encourage the children to attend and see if the church adults can do as well as the Guardians.)

Ask everyone to stand and form two big equal circles, one just inside the other. Ask those in the outer circle to do a half-turn to the left; those in the inner circle do a half-turn to the right. Now everyone should be facing someone, in the other circle. Explain what to do: you will all say the verse together while walking round the circle in the direction you are now facing. On each word, grasp the hand of the person facing you (right hands on the first word; left hands on the next) and cross over circles as you go, weaving in and out of each other. Say the verse slowly, while you get the weaving-route working smoothly; then speed up or slow down, whisper, shout or sing, for variety.

Invite the members of one Company to come forward and lead the actions as you all sing the *Learn and remember* verse song 'God is Love' a couple of times.

GUARDIANS' GOLD

The interview today could be done in several ways:

⊕ Interview an Elder Guardian who tells others the good news about Jesus: why do they do that? Are others pleased to hear the good news? Why do they think it's important to keep telling people about Jesus?

⊕ Interview an Elder Guardian who has not been a Christian very long or who discovered the good news about Jesus in an unusual way or with no previous faith connections. How has meeting Jesus been 'good news' for them?

In each case ask: What does this story about Jesus feeding the 5,000 mean to you? Why is it important to you that Jesus said he was 'the bread of life'? What do you think this really means? What is the 'treasure' in your relationship with Jesus?

UNLOCK THE TREASURE
🕐 45 MINUTES IN SMALL GROUPS

VICTUALS

Make sure the children are comfortable as they settle for refreshments. As this is the last day, you could provide special party food of some sort. As you eat and drink, say that you are going to go round the circle so that each person can share what has been the best bit about **GUARDIANS OF ANCORA** and what one thing they have learnt about Jesus. Give them some suggestions if you think some children will find this a challenge.

TREASURE MAP: BIBLE DISCOVERY

With older children (8 to 11s)

Ask the children what their favourite foods are. What is their favourite sweet food? What is their favourite savoury food? What is their favourite drink?

Encourage everyone to find page 36 in their *Guardian's Journal* or John 6 in their Bible, and read verses 1–15. Say that today's Quest is about another of Jesus' miracles, but this time it's not about someone being healed. This time it's about food! This story took place on the shores of the Sea of Galilee. Look together at a map and show the children where to find this area.

It is unlikely that the children will be able to imagine what a crowd of 5,000 people (or more!) might look like. You may find it helps to explain to the children how many times you could fill your meeting space with a crowd this size, or perhaps use an image that they will understand. For example, 5,000 people would fit on 79 double-decker buses. Once the children have grasped the size of the crowd that was following Jesus, ask them how they would have felt to have all those people coming towards them. How would they feel about making lunch for all these people? How many trips to the local supermarket do they think they would need to make?

Ask the children if they can remember where Jesus got the bread and fish from in the story. Jesus did amazing things with just five loaves and two fish. With a tiny amount of food he fed 5,000 people and he had 12 baskets left over! Encourage the children to say what they think about this story. What small things might they be able to give to Jesus that he could do amazing things with? You might like to focus this discussion around the special Guardian skills of the children in your group. How might Jesus use their special skills?

Read together John 6:25–35 (page 38 of *Guardian's Journal*). In these verses, Jesus says that he is 'the bread of life'. Ask the children what they think he meant by this. Did he mean that he would be eaten? Or did he mean something else? Remind the children that Jesus wants to provide for them and give them everything they need.

Summarise all the stories you have heard so far at your **GUARDIANS OF ANCORA** holiday club and ask the children to think about all the things they have learnt about Jesus. Take a few moments to talk about how amazing Jesus is, how much he loves each and every child in your Company and how much he wants them to follow him.

Point out the pages in *Guardian's Journal* where there is more about becoming a friend of Jesus and be available if any of the children want to talk about this further.

With younger children (5 to 8s)
Ask the children to describe their favourite foods to each other, and then ask them if they like bread and fish. What kinds of bread and fish do they like, or dislike?

Ask who the **Story of the Saga** was about today. Some children may have heard this story before, but it may be completely new for others. What can they remember about the story? Where did Jesus get the bread and fish from? How many people were fed? How many baskets of food were left over? Explain that Jesus was able to feed 5,000 people with just a tiny amount of food because he is powerful. He is powerful because he is God's Son. The little boy only had five loaves and two fish, but Jesus took it and did something amazing with it.

Read John 6:1–15 from *Guardian's Stories* pages 22 and 23 or your Bibles. Why were the disciples worried? What had they not realised about Jesus? How might you feel if you had been there? Encourage the children to put their reactions into their own words.

Read John 6:25–35 from *Guardian's Stories* page 24 or your Bibles. Emphasise the words of Jesus, 'I am the bread of life'. Ask the children what they think of these words. What does Jesus mean? Explain to the children that when Jesus describes himself as 'the bread of life', one of things he means is

that he will be like food for us. We need food to survive, and Jesus is saying we need him too.

Encourage the children to complete the postcard on *Guardian's Stories* page 25, or draw a picture and message on a piece of paper to express their own response to this story.

With all ages
Adapt these questions to suit your group, sharing your own feelings, opinions and experiences as appropriate (some are also in *Guardian's Journal* but are open-ended, with no right or wrong answer, so can be answered at any age):
⊕ What have you discovered that you didn't know before?
⊕ Has this story reminded you of anything you already knew?
⊕ What do you want to think about some more?
⊕ What does this story tell you about God?
⊕ How are the characters in this story like you or someone you know?
⊕ How do you feel after hearing this?

Encourage any child who wants to know more about following Jesus to talk with you or suggest who else they might like to talk with.

ORISON
As a light in the darkness, a lighted candle acts as a sign of God's presence, and many people see the act of lighting as a prayer in itself. In older traditions, people would pray – aloud or silently – all the time a candle was alight.

Children and candles can mix, but do take sensible precautions: clarify the safety rules and check with your safety officer beforehand. Prepare a safe, fireproof area where the children will be able to see the candle easily, without touching it; settle them in place before lighting. (If fire regulations mean you cannot have candles on the premises, choose another focal point, such as a beautiful and unusual flower or a picture that shows the wonder of God.)

Say the *Learn and remember* verse aloud together or read the words of Jesus from John 8:12: '…he said, "I am the light for the world! Follow me, and you won't be walking in the dark. You will have the light that gives life."' Light the candle. Often this action in itself quietens the room and draws everyone's attention, giving a sense of beauty and inspiring stillness. Children learn and experience through their

USING THE
GUARDIANS OF ANCORA
APP WITH THIS QUEST

If you have access to a tablet and are able to download the **GUARDIANS OF ANCORA** app there are several ways you could use this to enhance today's quest.
⊕ If you are able to connect your tablet to a projector, you could play through relevant parts of 'Jesus feeds a crowd' as a way of introducing the story to the children.
⊕ If you have enough tablets to have one per company you could encourage children to take it turns playing through 'Jesus feeds a crowd' at appropriate points in your programme. You might like to set a time limit to make sure everyone gets a turn.

If you have enough tablets for one company to have one each, you could incorporate time during construction or games for companies to rotate and play through 'Jesus feeds a crowd' in a dedicated 'tablet zone' under supervision. You could suggest the following to the children:
⊕ There are too many people for you to see Jesus: you'll have to find another way.
⊕ See what Jesus is doing – and what people think about it all.
⊕ What could you do to help out?

If you don't have access to a tablet, and aren't able to download the **GUARDIANS OF ANCORA** app yourself, don't worry, there are still plenty of exciting ways to engage with **GUARDIANS OF ANCORA**. You can start by visiting www.guardiansofancora.com to find out more!

Remember to encourage the children who attend your group to download the app for themselves if they have access to a tablet at home.

senses, and the contrast of light and darkness can be powerful.

Invite the children to think about their Bible discoveries today and pray quietly as the candle burns. (Many children are unused to stillness, so don't extend this time if they are not coping.)

Spend a few more moments praying quietly, and then extinguish the candles.

CONSTRUCTION

Choose a construction activity from the Treasure Store pages 80 to 83. There are craft ideas based on the **GUARDIANS OF ANCORA** theme and on the Bible teaching. Today's Bible construction is 'Fish butties' on page 81.

For extra craft ideas, see *Ultimate Craft* (SU 978 1 84427 364 5).

GAMES

Help the Guardians shape up by choosing suitable games from pages 84 to 86. There are extra themed games at the **GUARDIANS OF ANCORA** multimedia downloads area. For even more games ideas see *Ultimate Games* (SU 978 1 84427 365 2).

GUARDIANS' GATHERING
🕑 25 MINUTES ALL TOGETHER

TREASURE CHEST

Welcome everyone back by playing the **GUARDIANS OF ANCORA** theme song. Read out a selection of the jokes, messages, pictures and questions in the Treasure Chest today. Thank everyone for contributing to the Treasure Chest, all through the club. (If you are going to feature the Treasure Chest in Service 2, encourage children to bring their final contributions, or save some of the best jokes to use again.)

COMPANY SHOWCASE

For the last time, choose a Company and invite the Elder Guardian and two or three children to the front to show everyone something they have been doing in their **Company duties**. It might be an item they have made to decorate their space, an emblem or flag they have devised or a motto to say. Admire what they have shown and thank them for being enthusiastic Guardians.

THE SEARCH FOR THE GOLDEN SHIELD

Recap on yesterday's adventure, for anyone who missed the session. In today's episode of *The Search for the Golden Shield*, Swift and Dash meet some villagers and share the Story of the Saga with them. But will they find the story-treasure? And will Swift discover the greater purpose of serving the Story of the Saga? (There is a further scene in Service 2, but the drama will reach a satisfying conclusion today.)

KEEPER'S QUESTIONS

Divide the children into evenly-matched teams and devise a quiz that relates to all that has happened during your **GUARDIANS OF ANCORA** holiday club. This can include funny events that happened unique to your club (show images on the screen if you have been making a photographic record), as well as facts from the stories and the *Learn and remember* verse.

Alternatively, you can use the quiz from page 104 or from the **GUARDIANS OF ANCORA** multimedia downloads area based on the Bible story from Quest 5.

BENISON

Use the same method for your 'together' prayer time as for 'Guardian's guidelines'. Ask everyone to stand and form two big equal circles, one just inside the other. Ask those in the outer circle to do a half-turn to the left; those in the inner circle do a half-turn to the right. Now everyone should be facing someone, in the other circle. Explain what to do: you will all say the *Learn and remember* verse together while walking round the circle in the direction you are now facing. This time, though, say the verse as a way of talking with God, not as words to memorise: 'Jesus said: Love the Lord your God with all your heart, soul and mind.'

On each word, grasp the hand of the person facing you (right hands on the first word; left hands on the next) and cross over circles as you go, weaving in and out of each other. Say the prayer slowly, while you get the weaving-route working smoothly; then speed up or slow down, whisper, shout or sing, for variety.

(If you are not featuring the *Learn and remember* verse, you could still use this method but substitute a short prayer of your own instead.)

Say that the original fishermen that Jesus called to follow him were some of the first people to tell others about Jesus – and it's been happening ever since: 2,000 years of good news! Pray that each child present will be able to share something about the good news of Jesus with their friends and families in the coming weeks.

REVIVE!

The Firebugs lead the children in a couple of lively songs.

Round off **Guardians' gathering** by asking two children to say in one sentence what one thing they will share when they get home. Children are used to doing this in school. Elder Guardians can ask a similar question when the children are back in their Companies.

With all the upfront presenters together on the stage, have each one say a sentence about their **GUARDIANS OF ANCORA** experience: what have they enjoyed most and what have they discovered? Put all these 'best bits' together as you thank God for all the fun of the club.

Thank all the team and everyone who has been involved. Remind everyone about the collection procedure, the final service and any other follow-up events planned. If you run a holiday club regularly, remember to say: 'See you next year!' Sing the **GUARDIANS OF ANCORA** theme song one last time and then send the children back to their Companies.

SIGNING OFF
🕑 10 MINUTES IN SMALL GROUPS

Look back to the 'special Guardian skill' that each child recorded at the start of Company duties. Now, at the end of the club, ask whether any would like to change that 'skill'. Has being a Guardian changed them so that they have a new 'skill'? How do they see themselves, now? Affirm each child, individually, for being a fantastic Guardian!

RESTORATION: CLEARING UP AND A QUICK DEBRIEF

Once the children have gone, tidy up and if possible have a meal together as a celebration, with time to enjoy each other's company. There may not have been a chance for lengthy conversations during the club.

Encourage team members to feed back any comments they have about the club that will feed both into the wider ministry to children and the next holiday club that you run. Ask for feedback immediately, before people forget. An evaluation sheet is available online.

Make sure everyone knows about your end-of-club service, if you are having one, or about future team meetings and events.

Thank everyone for all they have contributed! Pray together, giving praise and thanks for all the good things that have happened.

SERVICE 11
LOVE THE **LORD!**

KEY PASSAGES
Mark 12:28–34; Matthew 22:37

KEY STORYLINES
⊕ Two volunteer Guardians find five balloons, which remind us of how important it is to love God with all that we are and have.

⊕ Jesus has shown us how much he loves us and he invites us to love him in return. Part of loving Jesus is showing his love to others.

⊕ Loving God should impact every area of our lives - our hearts, minds and strength - as the Guardians will have memorised in their *Learn and remember* verse.

KEY AIMS
⊕ To be excited about loving Jesus and following him.

⊕ To recognise Jesus' love for us and his call for us to love others.

⊕ To share with the rest of the church family what has been happening in the holiday club.

⊕ To welcome any children and their associated adults who have been part of the club but do not usually come to a service.

⊕ To be confident that the treasures of these stories will continue to be with us, even now the holiday club is over.

BACKGROUND (CHILDREN AND THEIR FAMILIES)

NO CHURCH BACKGROUND
Children who have come all week still often find it a bit of a shock coming to a church service. They may expect it to be the same as the holiday club, but no matter how hard we try, it will seem very different to them. Early in the service make sure familiar friends are involved and familiar activities included. Make it as much part of the holiday club as you can.

CHURCH CHILDREN
These children are used to church – so surprise them by how much like the holiday club it is! Make it the best service they have ever been to! Be sure to include as many of their favourite things from the holiday club as you can – songs, verses, seeking for treasure, as well as a Bible message that brings a challenge to Jesus' followers.

FROM OTHER FAITHS
Encourage the children to invite their families to this service. Use the word 'families' rather than parents since in many cultures families operate as a family unit which can be quite large. So don't be surprised if the whole family comes along (parents, siblings, aunties, grandpa and so on). Have people of different ages ready to welcome them. Make sure they have seats, especially the adults. Think carefully about how to build on the relationships you have made with these children and their families. People need to be around to invite them to other appropriate events such as parents' and toddlers' group, old people's day club or family fun events.

WITH ADDITIONAL NEEDS
Think about the family situations. Now that you have a good relationship with the child, how can you, as a church or as an individual, support the family in the future? This could be through babysitting, listening, providing meals, washing, shopping or being a befriender in a regular children's group.

SERVICE PREPARATION

WHAT-YOU-NEED CHECKLIST:

- [ ] Introductory PowerPoint (available from the **GUARDIANS OF ANCORA** multimedia downloads area)
- [ ] Drama script from page 94
- [ ] A giant number '1', made out of card, or five number '1' helium party balloons
- [ ] Five ordinary labelled balloons or five long labelled cards plus a means of attaching them to the helium balloons (the balloons need to be hidden around your meeting space before the service starts)
- [ ] A large cake
- [ ] A large number '1' candle and lots of smaller cake candles
- [ ] Three large candles

SUGGESTED SONGS

- ⊕ 'Make me a channel of your peace' *Mission Praise 456*
- ⊕ 'Take my life and let it be' *Mission Praise 624*
- ⊕ 'Heart, Soul, Strength, Mind (Love The Lord Your God)' *Fuego CD* (see www.powerpackministries.co.uk)
- ⊕ 'With a prayer he fed the hungry'
- ⊕ **GUARDIANS OF ANCORA** theme song
- ⊕ *Learn and remember* verse song

THE SERVICE

WELCOME

The leaders should introduce themselves and anyone else who is playing a role in the service. Explain what is going to happen during the course of the service to reassure any visitors.

SET THE SCENE

Say that Jesus has shown us how much he loves us and he invites us to love him in return. Part of loving Jesus is showing his love to others. Ask two leaders to each recap one of the stories that you have looked at in the holiday club, when Jesus has shown how much he loved someone. How did he show his love? How did the person concerned go on to show how much they loved Jesus in response? You could interview each leader or use some of the props from the original storytelling. End by asking them, 'So who was most important to the person in the story?'

Explain that in the service you will explore how what Jesus said and did are the most important things for anyone following Jesus.

INTRODUCTORY ACTIVITY

Explain you are on a quest to find out what matters most to everyone present. You'll give people some choices.

After announcing each pair of choices, invite people to raise their hand to indicate which is more important to them. A rough count will indicate the more important. You may want to simplify the choices for younger children. There are not necessarily any wrong or right answers, but this is an introduction to Jesus' teaching on needing to decide what is most important in life.

Which is more important:
- ⊕ to be successful or to have lots of friends?
- ⊕ to love or to be loved?
- ⊕ to have a healthy body or lots of money?
- ⊕ to be top of the class or to be known as wise?
- ⊕ to enjoy adventures or to be a celebrity?

A PowerPoint is available for this activity.

THE SEARCH FOR THE GOLDEN SHIELD

Introduce the club drama: *The Search for the Golden Shield*. Explain that, during the club, you've been following the adventures of Swift and Dash, newly graduated Guardians. Say that it is time to meet Swift and Dash for one final episode. What have they both learnt? Will they both learn to love God through the stories of the Saga?

After the drama, remember to thank 'Swift', 'Dash' and all the drama team for their hard work throughout the club.

BIBLE READING

Introduce the reading as follows: Jesus is often debating with the religious leaders about what the ancient laws mean, going into the finer details. He sometimes really annoys them because he knows his Old Testament history and teaching and he places what he says in the context of God's big story of salvation. Sometimes he answers with a riddle. When people ask him a question, he listens carefully and seems to know exactly what and why they are asking. In this story, one group of religious leaders, the Sadducees, have been arguing with Jesus about a law that Moses had written centuries ago. Another teacher of the Law of Moses is really impressed by what Jesus has said. So he comes to ask Jesus his own question.

Mark 12:28–34 could be read with a narrator standing to the side and with Jesus and the teacher facing each other. These two characters could be dressed in simple middle eastern robes. Make sure all three can be heard clearly and use a version of the Bible that is accessible to children and those on the fringe of church, such as the Contemporary English Version or the International Children's Bible.

BIBLE TALK

How many parts of the body do we have more than one of? Invite two children to the front to count how many duplicate parts of the body people can name – eg hands, eyes. You may get some embarrassing parts and any medical people present could suggest more obscure parts!

Add we have only one head, heart, nose, mouth, tongue, chest, bottom etc.

STORY

Ask the children at the front if they would like to help you a little more by becoming Guardians for one last time. (If they wouldn't like to do this, ask for two different volunteers from the congregation.) Explain that you've heard there are five clues hidden around the building that will help us to remember something very important about today's story. Send the Guardians off to find the clues (balloons) and when they have returned them to you, thank them and send them back to their seats.

As you hold the balloons, ask if anyone can suggest how they might help us remember something from today's story. Wait for a few responses and then proceed with the story as follows:

Say that the religious leader in this story asked Jesus a good question. Can anyone remember what it was? – 'What is the most important commandment?'

Explain that he was referring to the laws that Moses laid down when God's people first left Egypt. These laws were to help them live in a way that showed they loved God, and meant that they could live together with one another.

Jesus answers by concentrating on one number, the number '1'.

Show your large number 1 or a '1' helium balloon.

Jesus said, 'There is only one Lord and God.'

Ask a child to help you attach the first balloon to the giant number 1, or a label to one of your number '1' helium balloons.

When Moses said this, their neighbouring countries believed in many gods but God's people were very different, believing in only one God. When Jesus spoke, those listening to him believed in only one God. Today, when we live in a multi-faith society and people worship many gods, Jesus' words are striking. Jesus who was (and is) God came as a human being. He knew there is only one God.

Jesus said, 'You must love God with all your heart' – and we only have one heart.

Attach the 'one heart' to No 1.

Jesus said, 'You must love God with all your soul' – and we only have one soul, which means everything that makes us what we are, our whole lives.

Attach the 'one soul' to No 1.

Jesus said, 'You must love God with all your mind' – and we only have one mind.

Attach the 'one mind' to No 1.

Jesus said, 'You must love God with all your strength' – and we only have one strong body.

Attach the 'one body' to No 1.

In other words, Jesus is saying that we have only one body and one life (or soul, meaning our whole lives) to love God, so we must love him one hundred per cent, with everything that we have, all the time. So how do we do that?

Jesus said he would never leave us. He wants us to really feel his closeness, not literally in our heart but in how we feel things.

Point to your one heart!

Jesus is God, and he went back to heaven to be with God the Father. In place of Jesus the Holy Spirit came to live among us. We could say he is 'God everywhere!' So, we can experience God's love for us. We can chat with him, when we are walking or running, at school, in the playground, in the bath, driving to work, going round the shops, watching football or even playing football. We must love God with all our heart, everything we feel!

Jesus wants us to fill our minds with thoughts that please God, kind thoughts, pure thoughts, right thoughts, holy thoughts, friendly thoughts.

Point to your one brain.

This has nothing to do with how clever we are. We can find out how God shows himself and speaks to people as we listen to or read the Bible. If we love Jesus we will want to hear from him.

Talk briefly about how God speaks to you as you read the Bible.

We must love God with all our mind!

Jesus wants us to use the strength of our bodies to do the right thing.

Demonstrate some of the actions your one body can do!

This means helping others, showing God's love to them. Looking out to be kind to those on the outside of our friendship group, those who are bullied, a neighbour who might be lonely, putting other people's needs before our own needs. We must love God with all our strength.

But Jesus also talks about other numbers. He talks about Number 2, when he tells the teacher of the Law about the second most important commandment.

Ask if anyone can remember what that was – 'Love others as much as you love yourself'.

When we know God loves us, we are able to love others. We will be like Jesus who cared for all the people we heard about this week. And God will help us. So Jesus is talking about far more than Number 2. He's talking about 3,4,5,6,29,87,403... however many people there are whom we can help.

Jesus ends his answer to this teacher of the Law of Moses by telling him he is not far from becoming part of God's family. This man now knew that the most important thing for him is to love God with all his heart, mind, soul and strength – one hundred per cent. But it is not enough to know this. He needs to put this into practice by loving God and others. The same is true for each one of us. So what matters most to you or me? (*Refer to the opening activity.*)

Light the No 1 candle, and all the other ordinary candles on the cake – explain these represent all the people we can love as we show Jesus' love to them. Invite the children to blow them out. Say that the cake will be cut and shared with everyone after the service, symbolic of our desire to show our love of and care for others.

LEARN AND REMEMBER VERSE

'Jesus said: Love the Lord your God with all your heart, soul and mind.'
Matthew 22:37

PRAYER

Set up three large candles and light one before you say each prayer. Children could be involved in reading these, if they have been prepared and practised beforehand.

Pray for the people currently caught up in a crisis situation.

Pray for people in your community in specific need.

Pray for yourselves as you love one another in practical ways.

You could conclude with the prayer of St Francis or you could sing 'Make me a channel of your peace', which some visitors may recall from school days:

Lord, make me an instrument of
your peace.
Where there is hatred, let me sow
love;
Where there is injury, pardon;
Where there is doubt, faith;
Where there is despair, hope;
Where there is darkness, light;
Where there is sadness, joy.

O Divine Master, grant that I may
not so much seek
To be consoled, as to console;
To be understood, as to understand;
To be loved, as to love;
For it is in giving that we receive,
It is in pardoning that we are
pardoned,
and it is in dying that we are born to
Eternal Life.
Amen.

GRAND FINALE

End your Service on a high note, as
you have been doing on each day of
your holiday club.

TREASURE CHEST

Use the Treasure chest today, as you
have been doing all week in the club.
There may be new messages but have
a few of the most interesting items from
the club, a few of the funniest jokes,
pictures to show and so on.

THANKS (AND AWARDS)

You may like to include a time to thank
everyone at this point in the service or
make it a feature of your refreshment
time, afterwards.

Work out and announce some holiday
club statistics, including:
⊕ how many children
⊕ how many team members
⊕ how many snacks and how many
drinks consumed
⊕ how many Bible verses read
(readings multiplied by number at
the club).

Be lavish with thanks, to:
⊕ the whole team, including those
behind the scenes and prayer team
⊕ the Guardians for making the club
so much fun
⊕ those who deserve specific thanks,
as appropriate (you could also
make some awards for exceptional
categories such as 'helpful helper',
'friend in need', 'design diva' and so
on – think of unusual categories).

LAST WORDS

Invite everyone to stay after the service
for refreshments and an opportunity to
see what the children have been doing
during the holiday club. This can also
be a time for the team members and
church leaders to meet up with family
members. It would be appropriate, in
the light of the theme of this service, to
ask people to help others by serving
refreshments, tidying up after the
holiday club or doing some minor jobs
around the church premises.

Make sure that everyone knows what
else is planned to maintain contact with
the children who have come to the club
who do not usually come (such as an
invitation to a reunion party during the
next school holiday).

Bring the focus back onto God: run
quickly and enthusiastically through the
Learn and remember verse one more
time, and make it clear what anyone
should do if they want to find out more
about what it means to be a follower
of Jesus.

AND FINALLY...

End with one last rousing rendition
of the **GUARDIANS OF ANCORA**
theme song.

TREASURE STORE

TREASURE STORE I

TELLING THE SAGA
THE BIBLE STORY
SCRIPTS

QUEST I

Today's Quest tells the story of Jesus calling his first disciples, asking them to leave their lives as fishermen and follow him. Involve the children as fishermen, using actions together to represent casting nets, rowing boats, hauling in nets full of fish and any other actions you can think of!

Jesus looked out across the crowd. There were so many people, it was like a sea of faces. And behind him? Behind him was a real sea, the Sea of Galilee.

The crowd pressed closer and closer. They really wanted to hear what Jesus had to say. And Jesus really wanted them to hear, too. But he also wanted to keep from falling in the water.

Then he spotted a couple of fishing boats and he had an idea. One of the fishermen, Simon Peter, was washing his nets. His brother Andrew was there, too.

Jesus climbed into Simon's boat.

'Would you mind rowing me out a bit from the shore?' Jesus asked.

Simon wasn't used to people just jumping into his boat. But he'd heard about this Jesus and could see that he was a popular fellow, so he agreed.

'Sure,' he said. 'Why not?'

'It's all right with me,' Andrew added.

So, sitting in a boat and bobbing on the water, Jesus talked to the crowd.

'I've been waiting to hear Jesus, for ages,' said a man.

'Me too,' said a woman, standing next to him. 'They say he's very good.'

'I can't see!' said a boy, bouncing up and down.

When Jesus had finished speaking, he turned to Simon and said, 'I'd like to do a little fishing. Let's go out into the deep water and lower the nets.'

Simon wanted to be polite, he really did. But he'd been a fisherman all his life and he knew how ridiculous Jesus' request was. Nobody went fishing in the day. The fish were all at the bottom of the sea, way out of reach.

'But we were out all night, Master,' he explained. 'And we didn't catch a thing. Still, if that's really what you want to do, I'll have a go.'

'It's all right with me,' Andrew added.

So out to the deepest part of the sea they went. Simon and Andrew lowered their nets. And as soon as they did, the nets filled up with fish, flipping and flapping and trying to force their way out.

'I've never seen a catch so big,' cried Simon Peter. 'The nets are breaking!'

'This is definitely not all right,' Andrew added. 'We'd better send for help.'

They signalled their partners, James and John, who came to their rescue as fast as they could. They pulled the fish up into both their boats, but the catch was so enormous that the boats began to sink under the weight.

The fishermen were all amazed.

'This is unbelievable!' said James.

'But it's happening. It's really happening,' said John.

'I don't know who this Jesus is...' said Andrew.

'But only someone with God's power could do something like this,' said Simon Peter.

So Simon fell at Jesus' knees.

'Go away, please, Lord,' he begged. 'I'm just an ordinary man, who does things that are wrong all the time. I don't belong in your presence.'

But Jesus didn't see it that way, at all.

'There's no need to be afraid,' he said. 'I want you to come with me – to leave your boats and nets behind. From now on you'll be fishing for men!'

So that's what they did. All of them. Simon Peter, Andrew, James and John. They left their boats on the shore and followed Jesus.

QUEST II

Use a story bag containing the following items (these could be wrapped to prolong the anticipation) in order, at appropriate points in the story (alternatively, project suitable images on a screen):

⊕ *a figure to represent the Roman officer*
⊕ *a figure to represent the servant*
⊕ *a stethoscope (to represent the 'doctor')*
⊕ *a large sheet of paper with a line drawing of a synagogue (or a church, if you prefer) on it*
⊕ *the box of a DVD/film title that contains the word 'friends'*
⊕ *the box from a word-based game such as Scrabble (for 'if you only say the word').*

Stand the Roman officer figure up.

The Roman army officer was sad, really sad. He was a powerful man, the commander of a hundred battle-hardened soldiers, who would do whatever he told them.

Lay the servant figure down.

But his favourite servant was ill, paralysed and close to death.

And, powerful as he was, there was nothing the Roman army officer could do to help him.

Bring out the stethoscope.

'I'm so sorry, sir,' said the doctor. 'There is nothing more I can do for your servant. They say the miracle worker, Jesus, is in town, though. I'd say he's your only hope.'

When the Roman army officer heard that, he sent some friends, Jewish elders, to ask Jesus to heal his servant.

The elders hurried through the streets of Capernaum until they found Jesus.

'You know we don't usually like Romans,' one of the elders explained to Jesus. 'Their soldiers, in particular.'

'But the Roman army officer, here in Capernaum, is different,' another elder added.

Show the picture of the synagogue.

'He's really kind to us,' said a third. 'He even built our new synagogue.'

'So would you please come and heal the Roman army officer's servant?' begged a fourth elder. 'The poor man is dying.'

Jesus agreed, and went with them to the Roman army officer's house.

Show the DVD box.

When they were nearly there, though, they were met by more of the Roman army officer's friends, with another message.

'The Roman army officer says he's not worthy to have someone as special as you to visit his house, Jesus,' one of the friends explained. 'Or even to come and see you, himself.'

Show the word-based game.

'But he does know how powerful you are, Jesus,' added another friend. 'And he knows that you only have to say the word and his servant will be healed.'

'He's a man with power, too,' said a third friend. 'He orders his soldiers to come, and they come. He orders them to go, and they go! Yes, sir. No, sir. No messing about.'

Jesus was impressed.

'Did you hear that, everyone?' he said. 'This Roman army officer is not even Jewish, but he shows more faith in me than many of our own people! His servant will, most definitely, be healed.'

Stand the servant figure up.

So the Roman army officer's friends returned to his house. And by the time they arrived, the servant was already well, again!

The Roman army officer was right. All Jesus had to do was say the word.

QUEST III

Each character in the story needs to be voiced by a different person. The storyteller is effectively the narrator. Try to encourage each person to imagine the feelings and expressions of their character and to add these in to enhance the words they are saying.

Jesus got out of the boat on the shores of the Sea of Galilee.

And as soon as he did, the crowds were there to meet him.

'Hello Jesus!' the people shouted. 'Welcome back!'

But there was one man in that crowd who was desperate to get his attention: Jairus, the ruler of the synagogue.

'Jesus!' he cried, 'My little girl, my only child, just twelve years old, is dying. Please come to my house and make her well.'

'Poor Jairus,' said a woman in the crowd.

'He does a very good job at the synagogue,' said a man standing next to her. 'I've learned a lot about God there. I hope Jesus can make his daughter well.'

Jesus agreed to help Jairus, and off they went, pushing through the crush of the crowd.

As they were hurrying along, however, Jesus suddenly stopped and said, 'Who touched me?'

'Master,' said Peter, 'there are people crowded all around. Many of them have touched you.'

'No,' Jesus replied. 'Not in this way. Someone touched me and I felt God's power going out of me.'

And just then, a woman came forward and fell at Jesus' feet.

'It was me,' she said. 'I'm the one who did it. I have had an illness for twelve years. I keep losing blood. No one has been able to help me. But when I touched the edge of your cloak, the bleeding stopped – just like that!'

Jesus smiled at the woman and said, 'Your trust in me has made you well. Go in peace.'

But some people were not smiling.

'This is taking too much time,' one of Jairus' friends whispered to him.

'We need to get going,' whispered another friend. 'We can't leave it much longer.'

And that's when a messenger arrived from Jairus' house. There were tears in his eyes as he spoke.

'I'm so sorry, Jairus,' he said. 'Your daughter has died. There's no reason to bother Jesus, any longer.'

But Jesus wasn't bothered. Not at all. He simply turned to Jairus and said, 'Don't be afraid. Trust me, like that woman did, and your daughter will be healed.'

When they got to Jairus' house, everyone there was wailing and crying and moaning.

'There's no need to cry,' said Jesus. 'The girl isn't dead, she's just sleeping.'

When the crowd heard that, they laughed at Jesus and made fun of him.

'Don't be ridiculous,' said one of the people who was crying.

'Only sleeping?' said another. 'The cheek.'

'We're professional mourners,' said a third. 'We get paid to come and cry when someone has died. Don't tell us who's dead and who's not.'

That didn't stop Jesus, though. He went into the house, along with Jairus, his wife and Peter, James and John. Then he took the girl's hand and he simply said, 'Get up, my child.'

And she did!

Her mother hugged her. Her father, too. They were amazed!

'I think she needs something to eat,' said Jesus.

So her mother made her some supper. And it was the best meal that family had ever had.

The people outside were amazed, as well.

'The girl's alive!' said one of the mourners. 'Can you believe it?'

'Since Jesus made her well,' asked another mourner, 'do we have to give the money back?'

'I would not have thought it possible,' said a third mourner. 'But there it is! I have to believe it. Amazing!'

QUEST IV

Today's Quest tells the story of a house full to bursting with people desperate to see and hear Jesus. Some people brought a man to Jesus who could not walk, carrying him on a mat. Since they could not get him in through the door due to the crowds they lowered him down through a hole they made in the roof. Involve the children as members of the crowd and people on the street giving them parts of the story to shout and attributing appropriate actions to their calls. You may want to practise these words and actions prior to actually telling the story.

There was no room. There simply was no room.

Jesus was teaching in a house in Galilee. He was healing sick people, too. And the house was full to bursting.

'OWWWW!' shouted one man. 'Get off my foot.'

'Sorry,' said the man squeezed next to him.

'Sammy?' called a woman. 'Where are you?'

'Here, Mum!' he called back. 'Behind the man with the big bottom!'

Some of the people were the religious leaders – Pharisees and teachers of the Law. They had come from all over the land to see what Jesus was up to.

'I came all the way from Jerusalem,' said one of them to the others. 'I say we listen carefully and find out if this Jesus fellow really has been sent by God.'

What the people crowded inside the house did not know was that there were people on top of the house, too. Four men had a friend who could not walk. They were carrying him on a mat, because he couldn't move. And they were desperate to get him in front of Jesus.

'I can't believe you guys are doing this for me!' said the man who could not walk.

'You can't move at all,' said one of his friends. 'And we couldn't squeeze you into the house. So we had to do something.'

'But tearing up the roof?' asked the man. 'The owner of this house is really going to be angry.'

'We'll fix it for him,' said another friend. 'It's the least we can do. We just need to make this hole big enough to fit you through.'

Not everyone was pleased with this plan, though.

'Hey, what are you guys doing up there?' shouted someone on the street. 'That's my neighbour's house. You'd better get down, right now!'

When the hole was finished, the four men lowered their friend into the room, in front of Jesus. The people inside cleared out of the way. It was more crowded than ever, now!

Jesus was impressed. These men trusted him and believed in his power to heal so completely that they were willing to tear up a stranger's roof. So he looked at the man on the mat and said, 'My friend, all the bad things you have done are now forgiven.'

The Pharisees and the teachers of the Law were shocked.

'Those religious leaders look pretty steamed up,' said a man to his friend.

'They think they know everything about God,' his friend replied.

All sorts of angry thoughts went racing through the religious leaders' heads.

'That's an insult to God himself.'

'Only God can forgive the bad things that people do.'

'Who does this Jesus think he is?'

Jesus knew what they were thinking. So he turned to them and said, 'Why are your hearts filled with such thoughts? What's easier? To say, "The bad things you have done are forgiven", or, "Get up and walk"?'

'Forgive the bad things someone has done?' whispered a man to his wife. 'Make him walk? I think they're both pretty hard to do.'

'That's more or less the point, dear,' his wife whispered back.

Jesus went on: 'So to prove to you that I have God's power and authority to do the thing you can't see, I'll do the thing you can.'

Then Jesus looked at the man who could not walk and said, 'Stand up. Take your mat and go home.'

And the man did! Right away. Just like that. He stood up, he grabbed his mat and he bounced out of that house, praising God.

'Thank you for making me well!' said the man who was no longer lying on his mat.

'Yes, thank you, Jesus,' said one of the friends.

'That was amazing!' said another friend.

'Incredible!' said a third. 'Oh, and sorry about the roof.'

But the religious leaders were still not convinced.

'The man was healed, I'll grant you,' said one of the Pharisees. 'But I'm still not convinced about the forgiveness thing.'

'I think we need to keep an eye on this Jesus,' said one of the teachers of the Law.

Everyone else was excited, though. They had never seen anything like it.

'So if Jesus healed the man,' said a man to his wife, 'then maybe he really can forgive the bad things that people do.'

'That's more or less the point, dear,' his wife replied. 'Praise God!'

QUEST V

Keep the children's attention and channel their energy at the same time. Divide the audience into three groups and name one group 'the crowd', one 'Philip' and the third one 'Andrew'. Say that whenever they hear their character mentioned, they must stand up, turn around and sit down again as quickly as possible. Although this sounds chaotic, it encourages the children to listen very attentively. Depending upon the size of your group and how much interaction you want there to be, you might also like to decide upon a shout or action whenever the children hear the word 'Jesus'.

Jesus and his disciples – that included Peter, James and Andrew – crossed the Sea of Galilee. They stepped onto the shore, near a little seaside town called Bethsaida. And, suddenly, there were people, everywhere!

'I'm blind, Jesus,' cried out a man in the crowd. 'They say that you can help me see.'

'I'm lame, Jesus,' said a woman, 'They say that you can help me walk.'

'My dad is deaf, Jesus,' a boy shouted. 'They say that you can help him hear.'

And one man called out, louder than them all, 'You can do anything, Jesus!'

The crowd was huge, and growing bigger every minute. So Jesus and his disciples – that included Peter, James and Philip – climbed up the side of the mountain that towered over the town. And the crowd followed right behind.

A woman stuck her head out of a window, 'What's going on?' she asked. 'Are they giving something away?'

'Looks more like a parade to me,' said her neighbour. 'Oi! Watch out for those flower pots!'

When Jesus reached the top, he sat down and looked back at the crowd. There were thousands of people, now, all over the mountainside.

'Is that thunder I hear?' a man asked.

'No, it's my stomach,' said his friend.

'I'm hungry, Mum,' said a little girl.

'Sorry, dear,' said her mum. 'I didn't think to pack any food.'

'Jesus can do anything!' said that man again. 'He'll sort it.'

Then Jesus turned to Philip, one of his disciples, and asked him a question.

'These people look hungry, Philip. Any idea where we can buy bread for them all?'

'Buy bread for them all?' Philip replied. 'That would cost a couple of hundred denarii, at least!'

'When I was a fisherman,' said Peter. 'I only made one denarius a day.'

'So two hundred is like half a year's wages,' James calculated. 'We don't have that kind of money!'

And then Andrew spoke up. There was a boy standing next to him.

'We do have this lad's lunch, though,' he said. 'Five barley loaves and a couple of fish. It's not much, I know. But it's a start.'

Jesus smiled. He knew exactly what he was about to do. And five loaves and a couple of fish would be plenty.

He told his disciples – that included Peter, James and Philip – to sit the whole crowd down on the grass. He thanked God for the bread and the fish. Then he started to break it into pieces.

The more Jesus broke up the bread and fish, the more there was. His disciples – that included Peter, James and Andrew – passed it around, up and down the mountainside. Everybody had as much as they could eat. And more! For when the crowd had eaten their fill, there were twelve baskets full of leftovers.

'Couldn't eat another bite,' said a woman, patting her tummy.

'BUUUURP,' went her husband.

'What did I say?' shouted that man, again. 'Jesus can do anything!'

'How many do you reckon we've fed?' asked Peter.

'Been trying to keep track,' said his brother Andrew. 'Gave up at five thousand...'

The people were so amazed by what Jesus had done that they couldn't stop talking about him.

'God promised he would send us a special prophet, one day,' one man said.

'His chosen One. His Messiah,' said a woman.

'Jesus can do anything!' a voice shouted above the crowd, once more. 'He must be the One! Let's make him our king!'

But Jesus didn't want that. He knew the people were only excited because he had fed them. So, leaving his disciples – that included Peter, James, Philip and Andrew – behind, he climbed higher up the mountain and went off to find a place where he could be alone.

TREASURE STORE II
CONSTRUCTION
ACTIVITIES

STORY-BASED CONSTRUCTIONS

These construction ideas relate directly to the Bible stories for each Quest, giving the children a visual reminder of what they have discovered each day at **GUARDIANS OF ANCORA**.

QUEST I
FISHING NETS

What you need
- Garden netting (the kind used for protecting flowers or vegetables)
- Coloured paper
- Green crêpe paper
- Felt-tip pens
- Scissors, glue, string or twine, sticky tape

What you do
Remind the children what the Guardians found that unlocked the day's story – fishing nets! Ask them to think of as many things as they can that they might find if they went fishing with a net (eg fish, seaweed, crabs).

Using the coloured paper, make some of these things together – you could use the templates from pages 98 and 99. Also, cut out some seaweed from the green crêpe paper. As you make the different items, talk together about today's story – what would the children have done if Jesus had asked them to follow him?

Once you've made your water creatures and seaweed, spread out the netting. You can either make one large net for the whole group or give each child a piece of netting so they can make their own. Fasten the fish, water creatures and seaweed onto the net using string, twine or sticky tape, to make it look like you have just pulled it out of a lake! Chat together about what Jesus meant when he said Peter, Andrew, James and John would fish for people.

If you have made one large net for your group, stick it up in your Company area.

QUEST II
SANDALS

What you need
- Stiff card
- Thin card in different colours
- Felt-tip pens
- Scissors and sticky tape

What you do
Before the session, cut the stiff card into the shape of the sole of a shoe. Make enough for each child to have two soles (one left, one right). Make them smaller or larger, depending on the age of the children.

Remind the children of the day's story – what did the Guardians find that unlocked the story? Soldiers' sandals! Explain that you're going to make your own sandals and then have a go at marching! Encourage the children to choose colours of card to use for the straps of their sandals and to cut that card into strips about 4 cm wide. (They'll need six – three for each foot.)

Invite the children to decorate the straps of the sandals. Then give each child two soles and tape the straps to the underside of the soles. Do this as the child holds the sandal on their foot, so that you can tape the straps in the right place (one across the toes, one across the top of the foot and one round the heel). Trim any excess from the strips.

As you create your sandals, chat about the story. What do they think of the Roman officer? If they were in the officer's house when the servant got better, what would they have said?

With all the children wearing their soldiers' sandals, have a go at marching around. Give the children some orders ('March!' 'Halt!' 'Turn left!'). Have some more tape at the ready to do running repairs on the sandals, and ensure the children don't have any trip hazards in their way.

QUEST III
HANDPRINT PAINTING

What you need
- Large sheets of paper (A3, preferably)
- Thick poster paint in different colours on trays (plastic or foil food trays are ideal)
- Clean-up and cover-up facilities (such as wet wipes and painting overalls)

What you do
Remind the children about the item that the Guardians found that unlocked the day's story – the collection of handprints. Say that you're going to create your own picture of painted handprints. Make sure the children have covered their clothes with painting overalls, old shirts or other cover-up equipment. Give out the

paper and show the children the range of colours. Encourage the children to create their own pictures by placing their hand, palm down, in the paint and then pressing it onto the paper. Help the children wipe their hands when they want to change colours.

As you work, talk about how the woman touched Jesus' cloak with her hand, and was healed straight away. Ask the children what they think about the story. How do they think the woman felt? Then remember how Jesus healed Jairus' daughter – he took hold of her hand and told her to get up! Think about that together, too – encourage the children to say what they think about the story, and about Jesus.

When everyone has finished, make sure the children clean their hands carefully. Admire your pictures together!

QUEST IV

WOVEN MAT

What you need
⊕ Weaving cards (available online or from craft shops, or make your own from stiff card)
⊕ Different coloured wool
⊕ Scissors and plastic needles (or plastic drinks stirrers)

What you do
Before the session, prepare the weaving cards by taping one end of a length of wool to the back of the card then hooking the wool around the teeth of the weaving card, alternating teeth at the top and bottom. When you get to the other side of the card, tape the end of the wool to the back. If you have a lot of time during your session, you could teach the children how to do this.

Give each child a prepared weaving card and show them how to weave a piece of wool in between the wool fixed on the card. Then invite the children to choose the colours of wool they'd like to use and help them to start weaving. If weaving proves too fiddly with just the fingers, provide plastic needles for the children to use, or you could use plastic drinks stirrers (the ones with a hole at one end).

As you work, chat together about the story. Comment that the mats you're weaving will be like mini-versions of what the man in the story had. Talk about what the children thought when Jesus told the man to pick up his mat. Explore this a bit further, engaging with the idea that Jesus forgave the man's

sins first, then healed him. A physical and spiritual healing!

This activity might take longer than you have available. You might want to carry on in the final small group time, as you wait for parents to arrive. Or the children can take home some wool so that they can finish it in their own time. Alternatively, weave in materials wider than wool, such as ribbon or strips of cloth.

You could also do this using strips of paper instead of wool – it would be a quicker, but flimsier, option!

TOY BRICK HOUSES

What you need
⊕ Toy plastic bricks, including roof tiles
⊕ Building bases
⊕ Plastic people

What you do
Have a go together at recreating the scene in the house using plastic bricks. Build the house where Jesus was teaching, fill it with people, then put a roof on top. Make sure all the children in your group get to give their opinion on how the house should look, what should go where etc. Build a little mat for a man to lie on!

Re-enact the story using the model. Tell the story together, taking the roof off the house at the right moment and lower the man down through the hole. Use this creative play to help the children explore the story further – what were the people in the story thinking? Why did Jesus say what he did? What did the healed man do after the story? The children won't have anything to take home after this construction activity (unless you are able to give the toy bricks away!), but this is a creative way to help them engage further with the story.

QUEST V

FISH BUTTIES

What you need
⊕ Bread (rolls, sliced bread, wraps – you could provide a mixture)
⊕ Tinned fish (tuna or similar)
⊕ Butter or mayonnaise
⊕ other sandwich ingredients (eg cucumber, lettuce, tomato)
⊕ Plates, blunt knives, food wrap
⊕ Hand-washing facilities

What you do
Make sure you follow health and safety guidelines, and are aware of any allergy issues.

If you're using bread rolls, ensure these are sliced before the session. Show the children the ingredients you have and ask them which ones they have already heard about at **GUARDIANS OF ANCORA**. Comment that Jesus had about the same amount of food as you have here, and he fed 5,000 men (not counting the women and children!). Explore that for a moment, so that the children can wonder about it.

Once the children have all washed their hands, help them to create the sandwich of their choice. You can help them mix the fish and mayonnaise together, or they could have just the fish and bread. Not all children will like tinned fish, so let them have whatever combination of ingredients they like. Continue to chat about the story, or just more generally, as you make the sandwiches.

If you have time, enjoy eating your food together. If not, wrap the food carefully, so that the children can take it home with them.

If you have a longer period of time (and access to a kitchen) you could make bread together. Find a suitable soda bread recipe online or from a recipe book – soda bread doesn't contain yeast and so needs no kneading or proving.

QUESTS II, III AND IV

GET WELL SOON CARDS

What you need
- Thin card in different colours
- Felt-tip pens
- Scissors, glue

What you do

For the three quests where Jesus heals people, making get well soon cards for those we know who are ill will help the children process the idea of asking Jesus to make people better. It's a simple idea, but will help the children translate what they have discovered about Jesus into their day-to-day lives.

Give the group a few minutes to think about who they might want to make a card for. Invite the children to choose the colour of card they would like to use, then choose an image from the day's story to put on the front. They could use the day's artefact (sandals, a handprint or a mat) and draw that on the front of the card (or cut it out of card and stick it on). Or the children might have another idea.

Encourage everyone to write 'Get well soon' on the front, and then think about what they might want to write inside. This might be the Bible reference of the story, a message saying that you're praying for them or a simple sentence saying that they hope the person will feel better soon.

As you work, talk about how Jesus healed the person in the story. Why did he do it? How did it change that person's life? If you have a story about Jesus healing someone in your life (or you!), and it's appropriate for you to share with the children, do so. Be sensitive if children have family or friends who have died from an illness, or if they prayed for someone and they didn't get better. Think before the session starts about how you are going to address this.

ANCORA-BASED CONSTRUCTIONS

Help children get more into the theme of **GUARDIANS OF ANCORA** by using these construction activities.

MAP OF ANCORA

What you need
- Large sheets of paper (such as flip chart or lining paper)
- Art materials (paint, felt-tip pens, collage materials)

What you do

This is a construction activity that can be done over the whole club, or just in one session. It can also be done individually, or jointly as a Company. Talk about the places in Ancora you have heard about so far – the Guild, the Hall of Memory, the Theatre and the Spire of Light, the waterways and aquavators. Draw a map of what you think Ancora might look like. Include all these venues, but also anything else you think might be there – what about shops or a market? A harbour?

If you're working together, decide who's going to draw what and where on the paper. If some children don't like (or don't think they're good at) drawing, pair them with those that do, so that they can work with them, colouring in or sticking decoration on the picture.

If you're doing this across more than one day, add in any new places in Ancora you hear about each day and invent new places to go on your map. Decide where Fabula, Swift and the others live and spend their time.

At the end of the week, make an exhibition of all the maps that the Companies have created, particularly if you're having a Service at the end of the club.

Although there is an existing map of Ancora (page 96) encourage the children to create their own Ancora map without reference to this.

SPIRE OF LIGHT

What you need
- Boxes of various shapes and sizes
- Fairy lights (battery or mains powered)
- White or yellow paint and paintbrushes
- Fabric of various colours
- Coloured paper
- Scissors, glue, sticky tape

What you do

Work together to create a Spire of Light for your Company area. You can do this every day at **GUARDIANS OF ANCORA**, or create the whole thing on one day. Create the body of the spire by sticking together the boxes in any way you like. You could create a uniform Spire, or go for something a bit more haphazard and organic! If you are spending the whole club making the Spire, then you could papier mâché the whole tower using strips of white paper and PVA glue or flour and water paste. Leave this to dry until the next time you meet.

Paint the whole tower and, when it's dry, hang the fairy lights from the top, taping the strings in place down the body of the tower. Make sure that the battery packs or plugs are accessible at the bottom of the tower so that you can reach them to turn the lights on!

Decorate the tower using the coloured paper and fabric, making sure that you can still see the fairy lights. Then position the tower safely in your Company area. It might be worthwhile weighting the bottom of the tower by putting bags of sand, sugar or rice in the bottom box.

INDIVIDUAL SPIRE OF LIGHT

What you need
- Crisp tubes (or similar)
- Clear plastic containers (such as a large drinks cup)
- White, light yellow or beige paper
- Art materials (paint, felt-tip pens, collage materials)
- Cheap torches (optional)
- Scissors, sticky tape, glue, masking tape

What you do

Before the session, ensure that the open end of the plastic containers you have fits over the mouth of the crisp tubes.

Give each child a crisp tube and show them how to cover the cylindrical part of it with the light-coloured paper. Encourage them to decorate the tube so that it looks like it could be the Spire of Light in Ancora. Once they have finished, if you're using them, put a torch (light pointing upwards) in each tube. Tape the plastic container upside-down over the mouth of the tube using masking tape (so that you can take the container off and turn off the torch!). If you're not using a torch, tell the children that they can put a torch inside when they get home (remind them not to use a candle!).

Once the Spires have been finished, admire them all and talk about what the Spire in Ancora might symbolise. Encourage the children to give their ideas, and then tell them about Jesus being the light of the world (John 8:12).

FIREBUGS – 3D

What you need
⊕ Egg boxes
⊕ Paint and brushes
⊕ Chenille wires
⊕ Eye stickers
⊕ Scissors, PVA glue
⊕ Clean-up and cover-up facilities

What you do
Help the children to cut out two sections of an egg box. Stick these together, open end to open end (to make the body of the firebug). Try to use glue for this, so that you can paint the whole body. If glue doesn't work, use sticky tape or masking tape (but bear in mind that you won't be able to paint over sticky tape). Once the body is stuck together, encourage the children to paint it in a colour of their choice. While the body is drying, create the wings by bending two chenille wires into loops. Cut six lengths from other chenille wires and shape them into legs. Poke the wings into the top of the body and the legs in two rows along the bottom. Finish the bug by sticking eye stickers on the front.

If you have any other craft materials, such as feathers, pompoms or shiny paper, invite the children to use these, too.

If your group prefer large projects, create a giant firebug by taping boxes together to form a body. Make legs from thin boxes and stick those to the bottom. Make wings by twisting thin wire into loops and covering the loop with tissue paper. Poke these into the top of the body. Draw eyes onto white paper, cut them out and stick them to the front.

BUG LANTERN

What you need
⊕ Clear plastic containers
⊕ String
⊕ Ping-pong balls
⊕ Paint and brushes
⊕ Scissors, sticky tape
⊕ Clean-up and cover-up facilities

What you do
You can use any kind of clear container for this: yogurt pots, plastic drinking glasses or the bottom half of plastic bottles (pre-cut, with sharp edges removed).

Give each child a handful of ping-pong balls and help them to paint the balls different colours. This is a messy process, so make sure you cover everything up sufficiently (including the children!). If this will be too messy, you can purchase coloured ping-pong balls in advance. While the ping-pong balls are drying, attach a 15 cm length of string to one end of a piece of dowelling. Punch a hole through the bottom of a plastic container, thread the other end of the string through it and secure it with a knot or piece of tape. (Make one of these per child.)

When the coloured balls are dry, encourage the children to draw a face on each one to make firebugs. Put each child's 'bugs' into a separate plastic container, then stick that to one of the containers that is hanging from the string (open end to open end).

THE KEEPER'S GOGGLES

What you need
⊕ Cardboard tubes (the middle of a kitchen roll is ideal)
⊕ Bendy straws or lengths of thin elastic
⊕ Metallic wrapping paper or aluminium foil
⊕ Coloured chenille wires
⊕ Scissors, sticky tape, glue

What you do
Give each child a cardboard tube and encourage them to cover it with the wrapping paper (using one colour or creating a collage from scraps of different colours). They should then do the same to two bendy straws each. (You may need to use sticky tape, as glue won't stick well to the straw.) Cut the tube into circles about 2 cm deep. Stick two of these together, side by side, to form the lenses of the Keeper's goggles. (For older children, you may need to sandwich a length of straw in between the two circles, to form a bridge for the nose.) Stick a bendy straw on either side to make the arms

of the goggles. (Alternatively, use thin elastic – stick one end of a length of elastic to either side of the goggles. Make sure the elastic is long enough to be comfortable, but not so long that the goggles don't stay in place.)

Stick other circles onto the top of the goggles, as if they are different lenses that can be moved into place when needed – encourage the children to use their creativity. They could also make different optical options out of the chenille wires and stick those to the goggles too!

As you create, chat about the club, asking the group what they think of the Keeper of the Keys and the other characters in Ancora.

KAL'S TOOLBELT

What you need
⊕ Strips of strong fabric (something like hessian would be ideal)
⊕ Fabric glue and paint
⊕ Art materials (paint, felt-tip pens, collage materials)
⊕ Velcro cut into short lengths
⊕ Stiff card

What you do
Before the session, cut out different tool shapes from the stiff card – think of things that Kal might need to maintain the waterways of Ancora: hammer, pliers, plunger – use your imagination!

Give each child a length of the fabric and help them to measure it so that it fits round their waist, with the ends overlapping a little. Cut the strip to size and then stick one part of the Velcro to one end, and the other part to the other end, so that the child can easily fasten and unfasten the belt.

Using other strips of fabric, create pockets by folding the fabric in half and gluing two of the open sides. Then stick the pockets to the belt. Show the children the different card tools you have made and invite them to choose what they would like to put in the pockets of their belt. Encourage the children to decorate the belt and the tools then, when everything is dry, put the belts on and show them off to the rest of the club!

As you create, chat about the club, asking the group what they think of Kal, his twin the Keeper of the Keys and the other characters in Ancora.

TREASURE STORE III
THE GAMES

KEYS OF THE KINGDOM

What you need
⊕ A bunch of keys
⊕ Blindfolds

What you do
Blindfold a pair of players, while the rest of the children form a human maze with the keys at the centre. Invite one player to give directions to the blindfolded pair, who must keep together as they thread their way to the keys (and back again, if you want to extend the game). Swap jobs so that each group member has an opportunity to direct, seek and be the maze.

HUNT THE FIREBUG

What you need
⊕ Paper firebugs or other small items to find

What you do
Choose one child to hide the firebug (or other item), while the others are not looking. (It should be hidden without needing to disturb furniture or climb on anything!) Set the Guardians on the hunt, and see who finds it first. That player then hides it and you all play again.

Play the game the other way round. With one child not looking, hide the firebug and then challenge them to find it. All can join in with 'warm' and 'cold' as the Guardian gets closer to or further from the treasure.

SLEEPING FIREBUGS

What you do
The Guardians are looking for firebugs but they have all gone to sleep! All but two children are firebugs and lie down on the floor with eyes closed as if they are sleeping. The remaining players are Guardians: they move around the room trying to get the firebugs to move. The Guardians can't touch the firebugs but they can go close to them, tell jokes and so on to get them to move. (To ensure fair play, have an Apprentice watching carefully.) If a firebug moves, it joins the Guardians and helps them find more firebugs.

FIREBUG DRIVE

What you need
⊕ Pencils and paper
⊕ Copies of the firebug diagram from the **GUARDIANS OF ANCORA** multimedia downloads area
⊕ Dice

What you do
You can play this with the children in groups of two to four players; or make a giant copy of the diagram and all play together, with everyone's dice throws helping to complete the firebug.

Each player has a pencil and paper and starts by drawing the body shape. They then take it in turns to throw the dice and, depending on what number they throw, they draw that part of the bug on their paper. The antennae can't be added until there is a head, though!

(For children with shorter attention spans or to speed the game up, draw both wings etc or all the legs on a single throw.)

ANTIQUA'S SHOP

What you do
Sit in a circle. Tell the children that there is a market in Ancora run by a woman called Antiqua. She sells everything a Guardian might need – and plenty of other things too! Start the game by saying: 'I went to the market and Antiqua sold me a bucket.' The next player adds to the list: 'I went to the market and Antiqua sold me a treasure map and a bucket.' Continue round the circle, with each player adding to the list and remembering what everyone else has said. Give plenty of prompts, as the list gets longer.

TREASURE HUNTS

What you need
⊕ Clues
⊕ Treasures to find

What you do
There's a treasure hunt going on each day during Guardians assemble but you can play during your Company time, too.
⊕ Use the map of Ancora (page 96) to devise your own versions of 'We're going on a treasure hunt' (see Quest 1).
⊕ Hide a series of written or visual clues for the children to follow and find a treasure. Add quiz questions or challenges to each clue, to extend the game.
⊕ Fill a large sack with shredded paper or balls of newspaper; hide various 'treasures' in amongst it. Daring Guardians can plunge a hand in, find a treasure and try and work out what it is (without looking).

Coordinate with other Companies and make up treasure hunts for each other to follow.

TREASURE TRIALS

What you need
- Equipment for creating obstacles such as hula hoops, marker cones, wooden planks, a step stool or aerobics step, a play tunnel

What you do
Set out the equipment as an obstacle course, with each item relating to part of the map of Ancora. (To add to the authenticity, label each obstacle with the name of the map location or have labelled direction arrows pointing to the next place or obstacle.) The challenge for the Guardians is to find their way through all the obstacles.

You could play the game as a relay, with a new player setting off as the previous one finishes; or start players off at intervals, so several are on the course at the same time. Position Apprentice Elders around the course to re-set the equipment and to guide players on their way.

Obstacles could include:
- five or six hula hoops laid flat on the ground: players have to jump from one to the next, like crossing a lake on stepping stones
- marker cones set out as a slalom: players have to run between them without touching, like finding a path through the frozen forest
- a wooden plank, laid on the floor: players have to cross it without touching the floor, like a bridge over a stream
- steps: players have to step up and down ten times, like climbing the mountains
- play tunnel (or chairs draped with blankets): players have to crawl through, like going into a cave.

WHAT AM I?

What you need
- Blank card (roughly playing card size)
- Marker pen
- A timer (optional)

What you do
Together, think of people, equipment, artefacts and objects that go with the world of **GUARDIANS OF ANCORA**. Write each on a separate card. Shuffle the cards together and place them face down. Choose a player to start the game. They take the top card and hold it on their forehead so they can't see it themselves but everyone else can. They have to ask questions to try and find out what is on the card: answers can only be 'yes' or

'no'. Add tension to the game by setting a time limit of one to two minutes for each player.

GRAB THE TREASURE

What you need
- Lots of pennies or plastic counters
- Small bags

What you do
Scatter the coins or counters on the floor, as though a bag of treasure has been dropped, and give each Guardian a bag. When you give the signal, the Guardians must kneel on the floor and put as many pennies as they can find into their bags. Stop the game and count up who has found the most treasure.

Make the game harder: players can be blindfolded or only allowed to use one hand.

FIREBUG DANCE-OFF

What you need
- Sheets of newspaper
- Live or recorded music

What you do
Practise the sort of moves firebugs make: flap wings, wave antennae, wiggle body. Give each child a sheet of newspaper and ask them to spread it on the floor and stand on it.

Start to play the music while the children keep standing on the paper. Call out the actions (one at a time to begin with, but call several at once as the game progresses) while the children stand on the paper and dance like firebugs.

Pause the music. Ask the players to fold their sheet of paper in half and play the game again. If anyone's foot touches the floor, they miss the next round of the game but are then back in again. By four rounds it will be getting difficult! Have fun!

DRESSING UP

What you need
- Lots of pieces of fabric
- String, ribbons

What you do
Use whatever materials you have available to make Guardian costumes such as tabards and cloaks or bags to carry equipment and treasure. Tie pieces together rather than sewing or sticking so the costumes can be taken apart afterwards and used another time.

GUARDIAN, GUARDIAN, ANCORA

What you do
This is a version of the traditional 'Duck, duck, goose' game.

Invite everyone to sit in a circle facing inwards. Choose one player to walk around the outside of the circle, tapping each player lightly on the head or shoulder and saying 'Guardian'. At random, they should say 'Ancora'. When this happens, the first player runs round the circle, chased by the one who has just been tapped. If the first player gets back first, they sit down and the second player takes over saying 'Guardian, Guardian, Guardian, Ancora'. If the second player catches the first, the first player carries on as the one tapping.

GUARDIAN PAIRS

What you need
- 16 blank cards

What you do
Use large pieces of card if you are going to play this as a whole-group or whole-club game; or smaller pieces for a few children to play together on a table top.

Make two cards for each item of Guardian equipment, with the word and (ideally) a picture of each: spade, bucket, net, torch, rope, hammer, lantern, firebug. Shuffle the cards well and then lay them out, face down, in a 4x4 grid.

Invite the first player to turn over one card and then another. If the two cards are the same, that player keeps the pair and has another go. If the two cards are different, the player turns them both face down again and play passes to the next child. See who can pair up the most equipment; or play against time and see how quickly you can work together to pair it all up.

PARACHUTE PLAY

What you need
- A parachute

What you do
This is a game for a large number of children and adults together.

Spread out the parachute and ask the children to find a place around the edge. Have adult team members spaced fairly evenly around the circle. Go round the circle and give each person a word to remember. This can be an item of Guardian equipment (spade, bucket, net, torch, rope, hammer) or the name of one of the Ancora characters (Keeper of the Keys, Kal, Fabula, the Shiner, Guildmaster, Swift).

Ask the children to pick up the edge of the parachute and practise lifting it up high and pulling it down again. After the children have got the hang of this, lift the chute and shout out 'bucket' or 'Fabula'. All the children who were given that word have to run under the parachute and out the other side, before it lands on them.

Keep shouting out different words. Now and then, shout out 'Guardians assemble': all the children then run, while the adults keep the chute aloft.

RUN AND RESCUE

What you need
⊕ A parachute
⊕ A box of 'treasure'

What you do
Place your box of 'treasure' on the floor, under the parachute.

Encourage everyone to start to waft the parachute, lifting it high and pulling it down again (see **Parachute play**). Choose one child to rescue the treasure: when the chute rises, they must run under, grab one piece of treasure from the box and run out again without the chute touching them. Repeat with other rescuers until all the treasure has been collected. (You may want to play again so other children have a turn to run-and-rescue.)

CAPTURE THE TREASURE

What you need
⊕ Masking tape
⊕ A large screen or room divider
⊕ Large sheets of paper (lining paper)
⊕ Marker pens
⊕ Shiny card to make two sets of 'treasure items' of varying sizes
⊕ Lots of red and blue paper circles

What you do
This game will take a while to set up, but it is always popular and is worth doing for the experience the children will have. It is essentially a giant version of the game Battleships. Play with two Companies at a time.

In your playing space, place your large screen or room divider across the centre of the room. On the floor on either side of the screen, mark out a grid of squares, six squares by six. Also write 1 to 6 down one side of the grid and A to F along the bottom. Draw out the same size grid twice on the large sheets of paper and lay them flat on either side of the screen or divider.

Make your two sets of treasure: make one the same size as one square; one the size of two squares; one three squares; one four squares; and one five squares. You can keep the shapes as long strips or vary the combination: just make sure that both sets are the same.

Position one Company on either side of the screen (they can hear but mustn't be able to see the other Company) and challenge them to place their treasures on the grid on the floor in front of them.

In turn, each team names a square (say, F2 or B6). The other Company has to say whether that square has a treasure on it (or part of a treasure) or is empty. The first team puts a red circle on the corresponding square on the paper grid facing them if they have found part of a treasure or a blue circle if that square is empty. The game continues until one team has found all the locations of all the other team's treasures.

HOLE IN MY BUCKET

What you need
⊕ Two buckets
⊕ Plastic cups with holes in or ladles
⊕ Water

What you do
This is a game to play outside!

Set the buckets out, some distance apart. Challenge the whole Company to work together to transfer the contents of one bucket into the other, using the cups and losing as little water as possible. The players can all run at the same time or take it in turns.

COMPANY CLAMBER

What you need
⊕ A hula hoop
⊕ A timer

What you do
Ask the children to stand in a long line and hold hands. Meanwhile two Elder Guardians or Apprentice Elders hold a hula hoop so it is sideways on. The whole group must climb through the hoop, without unlinking hands, as quickly as they can.

Time how long it takes and see if they can beat their own time, on a second attempt.

GUARDIANS OF ANCORA APP

What you need
⊕ Tablets (iPads etc)

What you do
Before the club, have several leaders (who are willing to let children use their tablet devices) set up the **GUARDIANS OF ANCORA** app on their tablet devices (or if your church or organisation has tablets of their own, use these devices) so the game can be demonstrated and played during your club time. (Do not register children via the app, but do let parental adults have the necessary information so they can help their children sign up if they wish.)

During games time, let pairs or small groups of children play, and watch while they find out a little about the game.

TRADITIONAL AND BOARD GAMES

What you need
⊕ Games with a treasure or adventure slant, such as *Enchanted Forest* (for 6+ by Ravensburger), *Labyrinth* (for 8+ by Ravensburger), *Guess Who?* (for 5+ by Hasbro); Traditional games equipment

What you do
A games corner can be a positive chill-out space during the liveliness of the club. Provide a selection of games for varying ages and appoint a couple of Apprentice Elders to help organise and play the games.

There are numerous examples of games that were played in Bible times and that are still used today. Provide equipment and someone to help with the rules of games such as: draughts, Ludo, mancala, solitaire, marbles, hopscotch, throwing and catching a ball, tossing stones into a hole, rattles, whistles, juggling and pull-along wheeled wooden toys. You could try two or three games each day or set them all out in a large space and have the children move from one to the next, in small groups.

TREASURE STORE IV
THE **DRAMA** SCRIPTS
THE SEARCH FOR THE GOLDEN SHIELD

CAST

SWIFT
Female Guardian, just graduated from the Guild. She wears the Guild uniform of brown top and trousers, and coloured cloak (*could be maroon, dark blue or dark green*).

DASH
Fellow novice Guardian (*written as male, but could be female*), he also wears the Guild uniform.

THE GUILDMASTER
Head of Ancora, an older man, who wears a fancier, white version of the Guild uniform.

THE SHINER
A smaller, strange-looking man, always surrounded by firebug paraphernalia. He wears voluminous, highly coloured robes and carries a bug lantern on the top of a giant walking stick. He also wears oversized glasses.

MENDAX
Chief Masque, enemy of Ancora, dressed in black, with a mask that covers his eyes (*but not the whole of his face – he shouldn't look too scary!*).

MASQUES AND VILLAGERS
Can be played by the same people. The Masques are dressed the same way as Mendax; the villagers should wear dark-coloured clothing.

SERVICE 1

SCENE

The Guild of Ancora. It is graduation day at the Guild. Swift and her classmate Dash enter, wearing ceremonial sashes. They are graduating and becoming Guardians.

Swift: I can't believe we've done it! Guardians at last! I thought we'd be training in the Guild for ever. Have you seen my 'Highest Achiever' medal?

Dash: (*Unimpressed.*) Erm, yes. Very impressive.

Swift: (*With false modesty.*) It's not everyone who can graduate top of their class, you know.

Dash: (*Sighing.*) Yes. I know. There was one subject you didn't come top of though.

Swift: Well, the study of firebugs isn't a real subject, is it? Those firebugs just look after themselves. Anyway, what use are they, I mean, really?

Dash: What, you mean apart from pushing back the dark and the mist and keeping people safe? You know, there have been studies saying that firebugs will protect people when they get in serious danger. (*Getting into his stride.*) The Elder Guardian has just done some research about firebugs helping people in sandstorms. He said that...

Swift: (*Interrupting.*) Oh, don't start talking about studying! We've finished! We've passed all our exams and we're about to become Guardians – do you know what this means?

Dash: What?

Swift: We've got the chance to recover some of the most beautiful and precious story-treasures Ancora has ever seen! Just think, if we find the best, we'll be famous across the land.

Dash: It's not going to be easy, you know. The Guildmaster said that there would be people who'll try to stop us.

Swift: What? The Masques? They won't stop me – I'm Swift! The Guildmaster told me I could be one of the best Guardians Ancora has ever seen!

Dash: Yes, I know. You've mentioned that once or twice. Well, 5,478 times, to be precise.

Swift: (*Ignoring him.*) Come on. We've got to go and get our official Guardian equipment! We need tool bags, cloaks, maybe some new boots...

Dash: Don't forget our bug lanterns!

Swift: Oh, will you stop going on about firebugs!

Dash: But bug lanterns are essential. We need to take them with us, so that we can light them and hold the mist at bay.

Swift: (*Not interested.*) Yeah, yeah...

Dash: Listen, if we don't have bug lanterns and we get trapped by the mist, we'll start to forget who we are!

Swift: It'll never come to that. The mist will never trap me – I'm Swift!

Dash: (*Mimicking her to himself.*) 'The mist will never trap me – I'm Swift!'

Swift: What did you say?

Dash: Nothing. (*Changing the subject.*) Come on, let's go and get all our equipment.

Swift: (*Noticing the congregation for the first time.*) Hang on, are you going to be Guardians too? That's great! You'd better try to keep up with me. I'm Swift! (*She strikes a heroic pose.*) I'm going to be the greatest Guardian Ancora has ever seen!

She does some fighting moves at Dash, who doesn't react at all when she comes at him.

Swift: Come on! (*She rushes off.*)

Dash: (*To congregation.*) I don't know why I'm her friend sometimes... Anyway, hope you're going to come to **GUARDIANS OF ANCORA** this week. Who knows, we might actually find a story-treasure! Bye everyone!

He exits.

EPISODE I

SCENE

The Guildmaster's office. He is sitting behind a desk (or table), going through some paperwork (the desk should be littered with scrolls). We hear a knock at the door.

Guildmaster: Come in!

Swift and Dash enter.

Guildmaster: Ah, Swift! Dash! Come in.

He stands, walks round his desk and shakes their hands. Swift greets him eagerly. Dash is a little unsure and does a nervous mix of a bow and a curtsy.

Swift: We're so excited to go on our first quest, Guildmaster! I can't wait to find out where you're going to send me!

Guildmaster: Good. I'm glad you're looking forward to it. How about you, Dash?

Dash: Well, I'm not sure. It's a bit scary, not knowing where you're going.

Guildmaster: It can be, Dash, it can be. But sometimes, being nervous is a good thing. I've decided to send you out together on your first quest.

Swift: What?

Guildmaster: It's your first time out in the Mistlands, so you need to look after each other. You'll be coming up against things you've never seen before.

Swift: (*Disappointed.*) I know, but I thought I'd be out there on my own, defeating Masques, finding story-treasures...

Guildmaster: There's plenty of time for that. But we all have to start out – I went out with another Guardian on my first quest, you know. Anyway, I thought you might be a bit disappointed, so I'm going to give you a choice of quests. I'm going to tell you about one...

There's another knock at the door.

Guildmaster: Ah, and here is the person who will show you the other.

The Shiner walks in. He is dressed outlandishly and carrying lots of bug equipment, including his bug lantern hanging from his giant walking stick.

Guildmaster: Shiner, glad that you could join us. These two are Swift and Dash. (*They stare at the Shiner in disbelief at his appearance.*) And these (*gesturing to the children in the audience*) are our fellow Guardians.

The Shiner turns to look at the children and almost hits Swift and Dash on the head with his oversized bug lantern.

Shiner: Hello everyone! Lovely to see you all. (*Looking at his lantern.*) Wow, the firebugs are really excited to see you all. What's that? (*Putting his ear to the lantern.*) You think these are the best Guardians you've seen?

Swift laughs. The Shiner turns to look at her. As he does so, he swings the bug lantern back again, causing Swift and Dash to duck once again.

Shiner: Something funny?

Swift: Firebugs can't talk!

Shiner: On the contrary. Why, when I was coming to the Guild this morning, they were saying how much they were looking forward to meeting you and Dash. And I'm pleased to meet you too – I've heard a lot about you.

Guildmaster: Well, the Shiner and I both have a quest to offer you. Choose wisely – both are dangerous adventures, but both will lead to an amazing story-treasure. Shiner?

Shiner: Thank you, Guildmaster. (*He searches in his robes and pulls out a golden scroll. He waves it enthusiastically at Swift and Dash.*) Mine is a quest to find an ancient bug lantern. It is older than much of Ancora, older even than me! I have heard reports that it has been washed up on the beach somewhere along the Shorelines, to the south of Ancora.

Guildmaster: Your other choice is to go in search of the Golden Shield of Ancora. We have heard that it is still in the possession of the Masques, who stole it from the Hall of Memory.

Dash: (*Suddenly worried.*) Masques?

Guildmaster: Yes, they are still very dangerous people. They want to keep all the story-treasures for themselves, and the Golden Shield of Ancora is one they want to keep their hands on. They are keeping it somewhere far away, in the Petrified Forest.

Dash: (*To Swift.*) I don't think we should go on that quest. Masques? The Petrified Forest? Far away?

Swift: Come on Dash! That's exactly what we should do! Who cares about a rusty old bug lantern? This is exactly the kind of quest I was hoping for – I can travel through dangerous places, defeat the Masques, bring back a beautiful story-treasure... (*She starts whispering to Dash.*) Besides, this Shiner bloke looks like a right weirdo. I mean look at him. (*She should say something here that makes fun of the way he looks – tailor it to the costume the Shiner is wearing and what he's carrying. Dash should look more and more uncomfortable as Swift makes fun of the Shiner.*)

Shiner: What are you saying? I can't quite hear you. My ears have never been the same since I went over the Cascada waterfalls in a canoe made of banana leaves and mashed potato.

Swift: (*Embarrassed that she might have been caught out.*) Nothing. We were just... er... chatting through what we want to do. Weren't we, Dash? (*She nudges him in the ribs.*)

Dash: Er, yes.

Guildmaster: So, what will it be?

Dash goes to speak, but Swift interrupts him before he can say anything. He is left open-mouthed as she talks.

Swift: Shiner, thanks very much for the offer, but we're going to go for the Golden Shield of Ancora.

Dash: What?

Guildmaster: OK, here's the treasure map. (*He hands Swift a golden scroll.*) The map will show you where to go. Trust its directions. And make sure you have everything you need before you go.

Swift turns excitedly to leave, Dash looks horrified.

Shiner: Don't forget your supply of firebugs!

Swift: (*Not really hearing what the Shiner said.*) Yeah, of course... Come on Dash! We've got a shield to find!

She runs off. Dash follows forlornly after her.

Guildmaster: Shiner, you'd better watch out for them.

They exit.

EPISODE II

SCENE

On a road outside Ancora. There are some bug lanterns mounted on poles along the back of the stage (these should be similar to the ones that Swift and Dash are carrying). There are also some big pot plants or branches for Swift to forage in. Swift rushes on, followed by a trudging Dash. They are both carrying bags or backpacks.

Swift: Come on Dash! What's wrong with you? Ever since we left Ancora, you've been a right old misery guts.

Dash: Oh Swift, this quest was a bad idea. It's our first adventure as Guardians and you chose the most dangerous one to go on! We should have picked the Shiner's quest – it sounded much safer for our first story-treasure.

Swift: What? A quest to find a mouldy old lantern? Not likely. We're off to find the Golden Shield of Ancora – if we find it, we'll be famous!

Dash: We've only just become Guardians. We don't have to be the best straight away, there's plenty of time.

Swift: Listen, Dash, the Guildmaster wouldn't have sent us on this quest if he didn't think we could do it.

Dash: But what happens if we meet some Masques? They're really dangerous!

Swift: I'll take care of them with my amazing fighting skills!

She does some fighting moves at Dash, who, as in Service 1, just stands there and waits till she's finished.

Dash: (*When Swift has stopped trying to take him down.*) Are you done? I'm hungry. What supplies did you bring?

Swift: What do you mean, supplies?

Dash: Food! Just before you left, I asked you if you had got our rations for the journey and you said yes.

Swift: Oh… 'Rations'. I thought you said… er… 'Fashions'…

Dash: What? Fashions? Why on earth? Wait a minute, what did you bring?

Swift pulls out an extravagant hat from her bag and puts it on.

Dash: I don't believe it. Did you bring any food at all?

Swift: No, but I did bring this wonderful kaftan.

She gets a wildly coloured kaftan out of her bag and starts to put it on. However, it won't go over her hat and she struggles. Eventually, Dash loses his patience and yanks both bits of clothing off her head.

Dash: I don't believe it. So we've got no food at all?

Swift: Er, no.

Dash: There must be some food around here. You look in those bushes for berries and I'll check to see if there's a village nearby.

He gets out the treasure map and examines it at length. Swift dives noisily into the bushes, rustling and shaking all the branches as she looks for berries.

Swift: (*Emerging from the plants carrying a handful of 'berries'.*) Success! These look delicious!

She goes to eat one, but Dash knocks it out of her hand.

Dash: Have you checked them in the Guardian's handbook?

Swift: Handbook? No, I left it in the Guild. We've passed all our exams, Dash, we don't need textbooks any more!

Dash: Those berries might be poisonous! Listen, have you forgotten all the rules we were taught at the Guild? I thought you were top of the class!

Swift: Oh come on, Dash. That was all theory. This is the real world – those things we were taught were more like suggestions than actual guidelines that we had to follow. (*She lifts a berry to her mouth, then thinks better of it, just in case.*)

Dash: Unbelievable! (*He pauses, looking out across the children to the back of the room.*) Oh no, it looks like some mist is on the way. We'd better light these lanterns. You do those two and I'll do these.

Dash goes over to the two lanterns on the right, Swift to the left. They open their bags and begin to put firebugs (play balls) into the lanterns. Dash carefully counts a handful into each lantern. Swift shovels firebugs into hers, putting more and more into each one so that she eventually has an empty bag.

Swift: Right, that's that done.

She shakes her empty bag upside down. Dash looks at her in disbelief.

Dash: Why did you put all your firebugs into the lanterns – there'll be loads more lanterns that will need bugs further down the road. (*He gets the treasure map out and shows her.*) We're going to run out!

Swift: (*Without really looking at the map.*) Oh, we'll be fine!

Suddenly Mendax appears. He is carrying an eye mask, but he appears friendly and smiles at the two Guardians.

Mendax: Ah, Guardians from Ancora! Greetings to you! You must be on important business – can I help you?

Swift: Yes, maybe you can.

Dash: Well, I'm not sure…

Swift: (*Interrupting.*) Come on, Dash. Look at him and use your enemy-detection skills. He's not wearing a mask (*on hearing this, Mendax hides the mask behind his back*), he's on his own, he's smiling and being friendly.

Dash: I still don't think…

Swift: Dash! You've got to make quick decisions to be a Guardian! Give me the map. (*She snatches it off Dash and shows Mendax.*) We're on a quest to find the Golden Shield of Ancora. We've been told it's been seen in the Petrified Forest, beyond the river.

Dash: Swift!

Mendax: (*Ignoring Dash.*) Yes, I think you're right. I've just come from the Petrified Forest, and I met a man who told me he had seen the most beautiful looking shield in a clearing, just about (*he points at the map*) here.

Swift: Wow! Thanks! Come on Dash, we're on the right track!

She runs off.

Dash: Swift! Hold on! (*He runs past Mendax, stops and looks suspiciously at him. Mendax smiles encouragingly at him.*) Wait for me!

Mendax watches them go and laughs an evil laugh.

Mendax: Right into my trap.

He exits.

EPISODE III

SCENE

The Petrified Forest – there are weird tree shapes along the back of the stage. From stage left Swift enters, followed by Dash, who is carrying the treasure map and looking uncertain. They are carrying the same bags as in Episode II.

Swift: Come on, Dash, we can't be far now!

Dash: I'm not sure we're heading the right direction. The map says we should have turned left at that last fork in the road.

Swift: But that man we met said the shield was down here. That map could be out of date!

Dash: I'm not so sure. That man seemed suspicious to me...

Swift: Look, I came top in problem solving at the Guild. We had the problem of not knowing the location of the shield and I solved it by asking someone who knew. Easy!

Dash: But did you see what he was holding in his hand? I'm sure it was a mask.

Swift: Do you think he was one of our enemies? Why would a Masque help us?

Dash: I don't know...

Swift: Exactly. Come on!

Dash: Wait!

Swift: (*Getting exasperated.*) What now?

Dash: What if he was trying to trick us?

Swift: Oh I don't believe it! We're this close (*makes sign with her hand to show how close they are*) to finding one of the most treasured artefacts in Ancora – think what this might mean! We can make a monument for the shield that will help people remember all about the Saga. And you're getting cold feet!

Dash: (*Defensive.*) No, but I think we should follow the map rather than some man we met by the side of the road.

Swift: (*Annoyed.*) Well, all I can say is that he was more use than that map. You need to stop worrying about doing things by the book and use your initiative. You've done nothing but moan since we left. (*She does a whiny imitation of Dash.*) 'Don't eat those berries, light the lanterns,

look at the map, don't waste your firebugs, we should have taken the Shiner's quest...'

Dash: Moan? That's not fair!

Swift: Yes, moan! You used to be so much fun. Now all you care about are stupid firebugs and lighting lanterns. Maybe you should go back to Ancora and go on the Shiner's quest right now! Let's see how you get on with that weirdo!

Dash: (*Upset.*) What? He's not a weirdo! Why are you being so mean, Swift?

Swift: (*Shouting.*) Maybe because I've just realised how much you're holding me back!

There is silence. Dash looks shocked and upset, then turns on his heels and storms off stage left. Swift is left on her own. It suddenly dawns on her what she's done and she starts to regret her words.

Swift: (*Looking after Dash, crestfallen.*) Oh. Well done Swift. You and your big mouth. (*Turning to face stage right.*) Still, I need to find that shield.

She exits the opposite side to Dash. Seconds later, Dash comes back on stage.

Dash: (*Shouting and looking round.*) Swift! Where are you? Let's sort it out! (*To the children.*) Where did she go? (*Leaders should encourage the children to tell Dash which way Swift went.*) She went that way? (*He points to stage right.*)

He runs to stage right and stops to check the map. Swift comes on stage from stage right, but she is looking at the back and doesn't see Dash. Dash exits stage right, without seeing Swift.

Swift: (*Shouting and looking round.*) Dash! Dash! Where are you? I'm sorry I was so mean! (*To the children.*) Have you seen Dash? (*The children tell Swift where he went.*) He went that way? (*She points to stage right.*)

She runs to stage right, but suddenly bends down to tie her shoelace. Dash comes on stage from stage right, but he is walking so quickly that he doesn't see Swift. Swift exits stage right, without seeing Dash.

Dash: (*Shouting and looking round.*) Swift! Swift! Oh, where are you? What? She went that way? (*He points to stage right.*) But I went that

way and she wasn't there! (*Ignoring the continuing shouts of the children.*) I'm sure she's in danger, but I can't find her. I know, I'll go back to Ancora and get help.

He runs off stage left just as Swift enters stage right.

Swift: Oh no, I can't find Dash. Oh, what have I done?

Mendax and three or four others creep on from stage right and stand behind Swift. They are all wearing black masks. Swift suddenly realises someone else is there and jumps round.

Swift: (*Shocked.*) Wh-wh-who are you?

Mendax: Oh Swift, you foolish girl. You've made a bit of a mess of being a Guardian, haven't you? All alone in a strange place with no friends, no firebugs and no supplies. (*As he says this, he takes Swift's bag/ backpack.*) Whatever will become of you?

Swift: Wait! I know that voice... the man in the woods!

Mendax: (*Removing his mask.*) Correct. I am Mendax, chief of the Masques. And you are in serious trouble. Look! (*He points out over the children.*) Here comes the mist.

The Masques exit laughing. Swift looks lost and alone.

Swift: Oh no! What am I going to do? Dash! Dash!

She runs off stage left, still shouting for her friend.

PHOTOCOPIABLE PAGE

EPISODE IV

SCENE

The Petrified Forest, as in Episode 3, but with a tree stump set in the middle of the stage. A couple of the lanterns from Episode 2 are at the back too. The kaftan from Episode 2 is hanging on the branches of one of the trees. Swift enters from stage left.

Swift: (*Half-heartedly.*) Dash... Dash... where are you?

She looks around - if possible start to play some forest sound effects: an owl, creaking branches, wind rustling through leaves - and draws her cloak around her. She sits on the tree stump.

Swift: I've been an idiot. I thought I was going to be the best Guardian ever and here I am, in the middle of a strange forest, with nothing to help me. No map, no firebugs and no friend. (*She starts to cry.*) What am I going to do?

She looks up over the children and points at the back of the hall. She is scared.

Swift: Oh no! It's the mist! If I get stuck in that, I'll start to forget who I am! If only I hadn't wasted all those firebugs - they might have kept the mist away from me.

She runs back and forth across the stage, not knowing what to do.

Swift: What should I do? Maybe I could hide behind this stump and I'll be safe.

She hides behind the stump for a few seconds, but then realises it's not going to help, so she stands up again.

Swift: No, that's probably not going to work. (*She looks out over the children once more.*) Oh dear, the mist is still coming. (*She looks around for inspiration.*) Look! My kaftan! It's from Ancora, it might be of some help.

She crouches on the floor and throws the kaftan over her head. She sits there for a few seconds before lifting the kaftan up and looking out at the children.

Swift: I don't think this is going to do me any good! (*She looks left and right.*) Argh! Here comes the mist!

At this point, people carrying grey cloud shapes come on from stage right and left and get closer and closer to Swift. They should make their clouds bob up and down, as if the mist is swirling around. As the clouds of mist get closer and closer, Swift crouches down into a ball.

Swift: Dash! I'm really sorry! Help me!

Suddenly a bright light appears in the centre of the stage above Swift - it is the Shiner carrying his lantern. The clouds of mist spin off stage, as they are pushed back by the light. Swift looks up to see what has happened. The Shiner takes firebugs (play balls) from his own lantern and puts them in the lanterns at the back of the stage.

Swift: Shiner! What are you doing here?

Shiner: Your friend Dash came and found me in Ancora - he said you might be in trouble. So I thought I would come to see if you needed help. It seems like I turned up just in time.

Swift: You saved my life! If you hadn't turned up, I would have forgotten who I was. All that training at the Guild, gone for good.

Shiner: From what Dash said, it sounds like the training had already been forgotten.

Swift: (*Looking at the ground in shame.*) Yes, I guess I got carried away. I thought I could do it all myself. I believed everyone when they said I could be the best Guardian ever. Now, I bet I get expelled from the Guild. I was tricked by Mendax and lost the Golden Shield. (*She pauses for a moment.*) I was even really nasty about you, Shiner. If I were you, I'd have left me in the mist to teach me a lesson. I'm sorry.

Shiner: Swift, we all get it wrong from time to time. You're safe now, and what matters is that you learn from your mistakes and put what you learn into practice. There's more to being a Guardian than just bravery and confidence. But I think you still might be the best Guardian ever, especially after what you've gone through today.

Dash: (*Rushing on from stage left.*) Swift! Swift! Oh thank goodness, there you are! Thought I'd lost you for ever!

Swift: Dash! (*She runs to hug him.*) I thought I was gone for ever, the mist nearly got me! But then the Shiner appeared with his shining bug lantern and drove away the mist. (*She pauses.*) And, Dash, I'm sorry about what I said. I was wrong to make fun of you and the Shiner and the firebugs.

Dash: (*Hugging her again, before she can say any more.*) Swift, I don't care! I'm just glad you're safe!

Shiner: It's good to see that you two have made up. When Dash told me what had happened, I wondered if you'd ever get the chance!

Swift: Yes.

Dash: Maybe now we can start looking for the shield again!

Shiner: I'm not sure you can. Mendax and his friends will have found it and moved it somewhere else by now. We'll have to start all over again, finding out where they've taken it.

Swift: (*Quietly.*) Oh. I'm sorry, Shiner. Sorry, Dash.

Shiner: That's no worry. It will turn up. And besides, there are plenty more story-treasures to be found. (*He pulls out a golden scroll from inside his cloak.*) You could always search for an ancient bug lantern...

Dash: Yes!

Swift: Of course!

The Shiner hands Dash the treasure map and points offstage left.

Shiner: And I think the map starts just over there.

They all rush off, with Dash and Swift chatting excitedly about the adventure they're about to have.

EPISODE V

SCENE

On the road to the Shorelines, once again, there are bug lanterns at the back of the stage, but the trees of the last two episodes are gone. Dash and Swift enter from stage right, chatting.

Dash: (*As if coming to the end of a long story.*) ...and then I found the Shiner in his tower and explained everything. He told me to restock my firebug bag, and then come and find you. But when I did, the Shiner was there already, and he'd saved you!

Swift: Dash, you did so much to help me. After what I said, I wouldn't have blamed you if you had done nothing.

Dash: Swift, I wouldn't have been much of a friend, or a Guardian, if I'd left you to get trapped in the mist! And while we were training at the Guild, I was a bit of an idiot – I was jealous of you. You were always the best at everything.

Swift: Well we know that's not true now, don't we?

Dash: You made some mistakes. So did I. But we're safe now and we've learned a lot! Come on, we're on a new quest! Let's see how far we are away from the sea. (*He gets the treasure map out and looks at it.*) Now, we're here (*he points*), and the lantern was last seen here. (*He points at a different place on the map.*)

Swift: Brilliant! Not far to go then.

Three or four villagers enter from stage left. (The lines for the villagers can be split up according to how many villagers you have and how many of them are happy to speak.)

Villager 1: Guardians!

Villager 2: They can help us!

Swift: What do you need?

Villager 1: The mist has been swirling around here and we've run out of firebugs.

Villager 2: Can you light our lanterns for us?

Dash: Of course! Come on Swift, you know what to do.

Dash and Swift go to the lanterns at the back of the stage and fill them with firebugs (play balls) taken from their bags. Choreograph a short sequence where Dash and Swift throw the balls to each other and to the villagers.

Villager 1: Thanks! We're safe again.

Villager 2: One of my friends got trapped in the mist once, it was terrible – it took ages for his memory to come back. He didn't know who he was or where he lived.

Swift and Dash look at each other.

Swift: I almost got trapped in the mist. I was alone in the Petrified Forest and I'd run out of firebugs. The mist was getting closer and closer...

Villager 1: Alone in the forest? Why?

Villager 2: How did you escape?

Swift: We'd had an argument and gone our separate ways. The Shiner arrived and drove back the mist with his lantern. Dash had gone back to Ancora and told him what had happened.

Villager 1: You know what I don't understand? Why do you Guardians put yourselves in danger, travelling all over the country looking for story-treasures?

Dash: Well, it's all so that we can discover more about the Saga.

Swift: Yes, the Saga is one big story made up of smaller ones, all of which tell us so much about who we are.

Dash: The treasures that we find unlock more of the stories!

Villager 2: Go on then, tell us about some of those stories!

Swift: Well, the children here have been hearing some stories at the **GUARDIANS OF ANCORA** club this week. Maybe they can tell you. What stories can you remember, Guardians?

The children tell Swift, Dash and the villagers what they have learned at **GUARDIANS OF ANCORA***. The characters on stage react accordingly.*

Villager 1: Wow! Those stories are worth hearing!

Villager 2: Yes, they're amazing! So, are you looking for a new story-treasure now?

Dash: Yes, an ancient bug lantern.

Swift: Dash, maybe we shouldn't say. Not after last time, when Mendax tricked me.

Villager 1: A bug lantern? I saw something like that down on the beach. It didn't look much, just something that had been washed up by the sea.

Swift and Dash look at each other. They are unsure whether they should believe the villager.

Dash: Could you point to where you saw it on this map? (*He shows the map to the villager.*)

Villager 1: Yes, it was just here. (*He points at the map.*) Oh, that's just where the map is telling you to go!

Swift and Dash smile at each other.

Dash: Thanks! Come on Swift, let's go!

They say their goodbyes to the villagers and everyone leaves – the villagers stage right and the Guardians stage left. While the stage is clear, an old bug lantern in placed in the centre of the audience. After a couple of seconds, Dash and Swift come back on again.

Dash: (*Checking the map.*) This could be the place!

Swift: Right. So where's the bug lantern then?

Dash: It must be here somewhere. Let's have a look around.

They both start hunting around the stage. The children will realise that they can see the lantern and start shouting about its whereabouts. Dash and Swift should interact with the children and pretend they can't see it for a while. Finally, they find it and Swift goes out into the children to collect the lantern. Back on stage, she polishes it with her sleeve.

Swift: Look, when you clean the dirt and muck off it, it's quite beautiful!

Dash: Yes! And I bet the story it unlocks will be a beautiful one too!

Swift: Well, we'd better get back to Ancora to find out! Come on! (*To the children.*) Bye everyone! Thanks for your help!

They exit.

SERVICE 11

SCENE

The Hall of Memory. The Keeper is behind her desk. Swift and Dash enter, carrying the bug lantern.

Keeper: Swift and Dash! How great to see you! I hear you've had quite an adventure...

Swift: You could say that!

Keeper: What happened?

Dash: Well, we were called in to see the Guildmaster for our first quest after graduating from the Guild. And the Guildmaster and the Shiner gave us a choice of quests – for the Golden Shield of Ancora or a rusty old lantern!

Swift: And I made the wrong choice.

Keeper: The wrong choice, what do you mean?

Swift: Well, I chose the Golden Shield because I thought finding that would make me look good. I was going to be the best Guardian Ancora had ever seen and I thought the shield was much more fitting for someone of my talents!

Keeper: Ah, I see. And how did that work out for you?

Swift: I thought I knew everything and it was going to be easy, but I made some bad mistakes...

Dash: And we had an argument...

Swift: And I was mean to Dash...

Dash: And I stormed off and left Swift alone in the Petrified Forest...

Swift: And I was tricked by Mendax, the leader of the Masques, and I almost got swallowed up by the mist!

Keeper: Goodness! That sounds quite an adventure. How did you escape?

Dash: I came back to Ancora to ask the Shiner for help.

Swift: And he came to my rescue just in time. He used his bug lantern to force back the mist!

Keeper: And so, did you go off and find the shield?

Dash: (*Sadly.*) No. By this time, Mendax had stolen it and moved it somewhere else.

Swift: Because I was so bigheaded and careless, we lost the shield. The Shiner said that we'd have to start our search for the shield all over again. We're sorry, Keeper.

Keeper: I think that's all right. It sounds like you learned a valuable lesson out there. We found the location of the shield once, we can do it again! But you've got something else there.

Dash: Yes, it's the old lantern! After the Shiner found us, he gave us the other treasure map and we found this story-treasure instead!

Swift: We also helped some villagers by lighting their lanterns, and told them about the wonderful Saga.

Dash: The boys and girls helped us tell the villagers about the stories they had heard at our **GUARDIANS OF ANCORA** club.

Swift: I wonder if they can do that again. Guardians, can you remind us of all the stories you heard this week?

The characters give some time for the children to tell them about the stories from the club programme.

Keeper: Well, it sounds like everyone has learned some amazing things this week!

Dash and Swift: Yes!

Keeper: And now, it's about time we found out what story is behind that bug lantern!

They exit.

TREASURE STORE V
OTHER RESOURCES

STRIPS FOR WORKING OUT **YOUR AIMS**

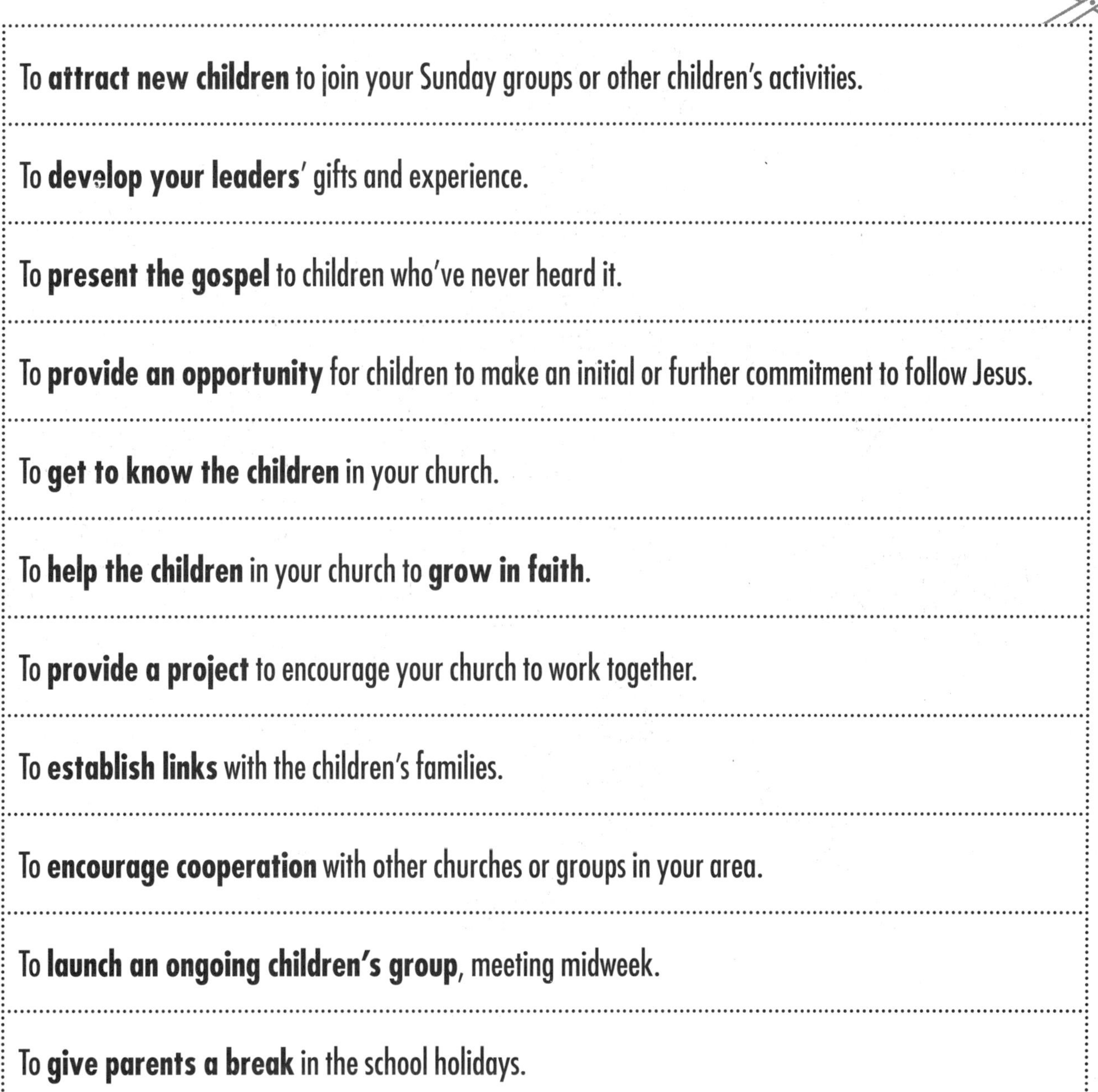

To **attract new children** to join your Sunday groups or other children's activities.

To **develop your leaders**' gifts and experience.

To **present the gospel** to children who've never heard it.

To **provide an opportunity** for children to make an initial or further commitment to follow Jesus.

To **get to know the children** in your church.

To **help the children** in your church to **grow in faith**.

To **provide a project** to encourage your church to work together.

To **establish links** with the children's families.

To **encourage cooperation** with other churches or groups in your area.

To **launch an ongoing children's group**, meeting midweek.

To **give parents a break** in the school holidays.

PHOTOCOPIABLE PAGE

MAP OF ANCORA

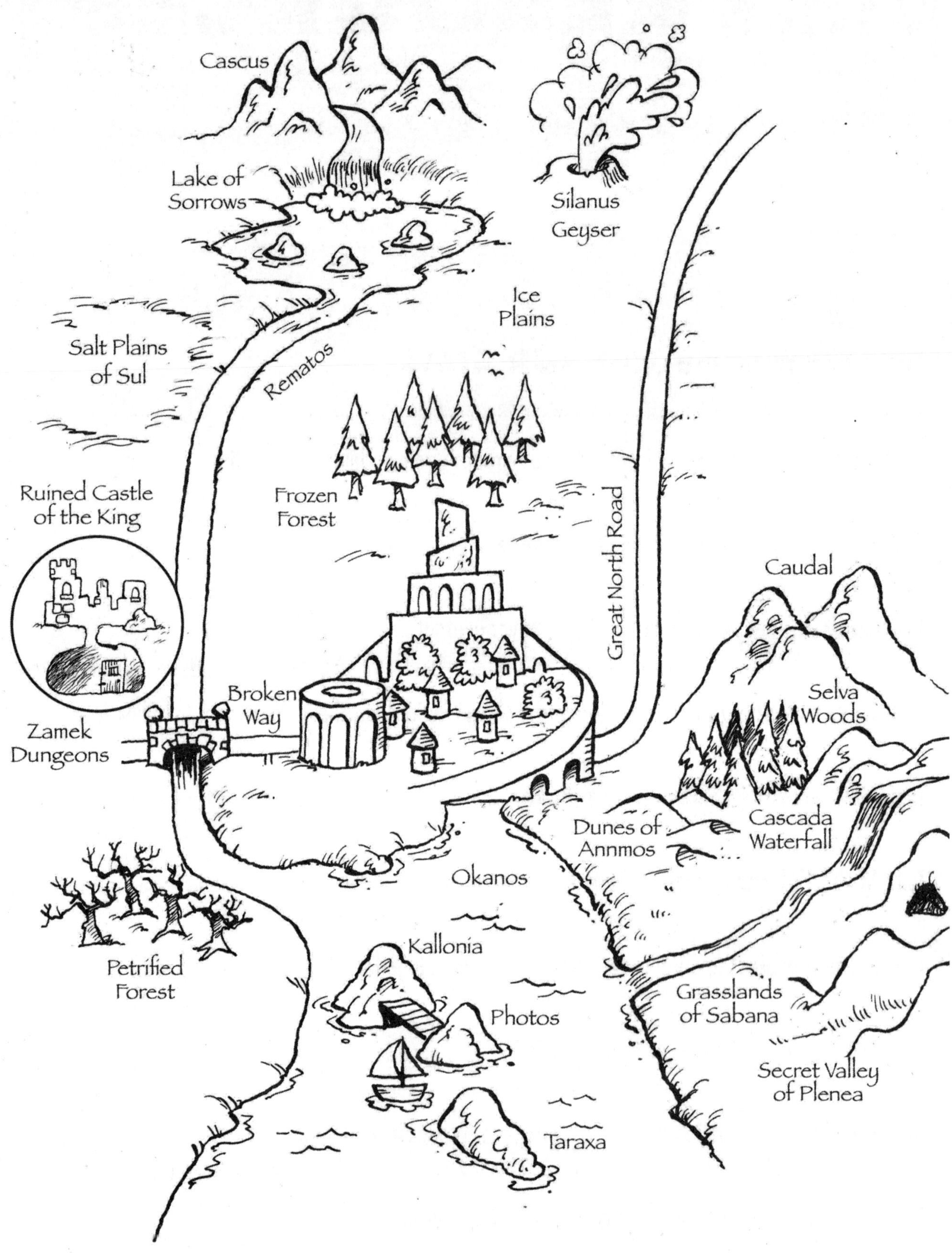

FIRE**BUGS**

TEMPLATES FOR **FISHING NETS**

TEMPLATES FOR **FISHING NETS**

QUEST I
KEEPER'S QUESTIONS

I Where did Jesus start teaching the people?

- [ ] **A** on the shore of the lake
- [ ] **B** on the banks of the river
- [ ] **C** on the seashore
- [ ] **D** on the edge of a volcano

2 Why were the two boats empty?

- [ ] **A** it was the fishermen's day off
- [ ] **B** they were old, broken boats
- [ ] **C** the fishermen were eating their lunch
- [ ] **D** the fishermen were washing their nets

3 What did Jesus first ask Simon to do?

- [ ] **A** row the boat away quickly
- [ ] **B** catch some fish
- [ ] **C** push his boat just to be sure
- [ ] **D** push his boat a little way from the shore

4 When Jesus had finished talking to the people, what did he ask Simon to do?

- [ ] **A** row to the other side of the lake
- [ ] **B** row out into deep water to catch some fish
- [ ] **C** row, row, row the boat
- [ ] **D** row to the other side of the lake to catch fish

5 Why was Simon not keen to go fishing?

- [ ] **A** he wanted to sleep
- [ ] **B** he wanted to listen to Jesus teach some more
- [ ] **C** he had enough fish already
- [ ] **D** he had fished all night and not caught any fish

6 What happened when they let down their nets?

- [ ] **A** they caught so many fish that their nets began ripping apart
- [ ] **B** they caught so many fish that their tummies started rumbling
- [ ] **C** they caught so many fish that they had to throw lots of them back into the sea
- [ ] **D** they caught so many fish that they never had to fish again

7 What nearly happened when they put the fish into their and their friends' boat?

- [ ] **A** their friends sailed off with the fish
- [ ] **B** the boats sank
- [ ] **C** the boats rocked from side to side
- [ ] **D** the boats nearly sank

8 When he saw what happened, what did Simon realise about himself?

- [ ] **A** he was a soldier
- [ ] **B** he wasn't Jesus' friend
- [ ] **C** he was a dog's dinner
- [ ] **D** he was a sinner

9 What did Jesus say to Simon?

- [ ] **A** "God loves you"
- [ ] **B** "Come, follow me"
- [ ] **C** "Now you will be catching people"
- [ ] **D** "I have a job for you"

IO What did the fishermen do once they were back on the shore?

- [ ] **A** they parked their boats and went for lunch
- [ ] **B** they pulled up their boats and left them to follow Jesus
- [ ] **C** they pulled up their boats and sorted out their nets into bags to take with them when they followed Jesus
- [ ] **D** they sold their boats and nets so they could follow Jesus

QUEST II
KEEPER'S QUESTIONS

1 **In which town did this story take place?**

- [ ] **A** Capernaum
- [ ] **B** Capername
- [ ] **C** Bethlehem
- [ ] **D** Caperbaum

2 **Who was sick?**

- [ ] **A** a Roman officer
- [ ] **B** a Roman officer's servant
- [ ] **C** a Roman officer's wife
- [ ] **D** a Romanian

3 **How sick was the sick person?**

- [ ] **A** they just had a cold
- [ ] **B** they were very sick and about to die
- [ ] **C** they were quite sick
- [ ] **D** they were very sick but getting better

4 **When Jesus heard about the sick person, what did he do?**

- [ ] **A** he healed them
- [ ] **B** he started to travel to the house where the sick person was
- [ ] **C** he prayed all night
- [ ] **D** he said he didn't heal Romans

5 **What did the officer do when he heard that Jesus was coming to his house?**

- [ ] **A** he cleaned it
- [ ] **B** he got his servants to make Jesus a nice meal
- [ ] **C** he told the sick person not to worry because help was coming
- [ ] **D** he sent a message to Jesus just to give the order to make the sick person well

6 **Which command was NOT one that the officer gave as an example?**

- [ ] **A** "Go!"
- [ ] **B** "Come!"
- [ ] **C** "March!"
- [ ] **D** "Do this!"

7 **Why did the officer ask Jesus to give the order?**

- [ ] **A** he understood that Jesus had authority over sickness, just as he had authority over soldiers
- [ ] **B** he understood that Jesus was a healer
- [ ] **C** he knew Jesus was very busy
- [ ] **D** he didn't want Jesus at his house

8 **How did Jesus feel when the officer asked him to heal without visiting the house?**

- [ ] **A** disappointed
- [ ] **B** sad
- [ ] **C** relieved
- [ ] **D** surprised

9 **What did Jesus say the officer had a lot of?**

- [ ] **A** faith
- [ ] **B** guts
- [ ] **C** soldiers
- [ ] **D** love

10 **When was the servant healed?**

- [ ] **A** by the time the officer got home
- [ ] **B** within a few days
- [ ] **C** very quickly
- [ ] **D** right away

QUEST III
KEEPER'S QUESTIONS

1 What was the name of the man in charge of the Jewish meeting place or synagogue?

- **A** Jerusalem
- **B** Jeremiah
- **C** Jairus
- **D** Joshua

2 How old was the man's daughter?

- **A** 10
- **B** 12
- **C** 16
- **D** 30

3 What was wrong with her?

- **A** she was daring
- **B** she was dying
- **C** she was diving
- **D** she was dozing

4 For how many years had the woman been bleeding?

- **A** 10
- **B** 12
- **C** 16
- **D** 30

5 What had she spent trying to get better?

- **A** all her time
- **B** all her money
- **C** all her prayers
- **D** all her blessings

6 What happened when the woman touched Jesus' clothes?

- **A** she was healed immediately
- **B** she fell over
- **C** she knew he loved her
- **D** she felt happy

7 How did Jesus know someone had touched him?

- **A** because they had cold hands
- **B** because he had sensitive skin
- **C** because he felt their power
- **D** because he felt power go out from him

8 When Jesus heard that the little girl had died, what did he tell Jairus to have?

- **A** courage
- **B** faith
- **C** blessing
- **D** dogs

9 Who did NOT go into the house with Jesus?

- **A** Peter
- **B** James and John
- **C** the people who were weeping outside
- **D** the girl's parents

10 What did Jesus do as he told the girl to get up?

- **A** he held her hand
- **B** he held her foot
- **C** he put his hand on her head
- **D** he knelt down beside her

QUEST IV
KEEPER'S QUESTIONS

1 Where had the Pharisees and teachers of the Law NOT come from?

- [ ] **A** every town in Galilee
- [ ] **B** every town in Judea
- [ ] **C** Jerusalem
- [ ] **D** Bethlehem

2 What did the men come carrying?

- [ ] **A** a paralysed man on a mat
- [ ] **B** a blind man
- [ ] **C** a large roll of carpet
- [ ] **D** a ladder

3 Why did they take the paralysed man on to the roof?!

- [ ] **A** to give him a better view of Jesus
- [ ] **B** to help Jesus see him
- [ ] **C** so they could make a hole and lower him into the room where Jesus was
- [ ] **D** so they could make a hole so he could see Jesus

4 When Jesus saw how much faith they had, what did he say to the man?

- [ ] **A** "Get up and walk"
- [ ] **B** "My friend, your sins are forgiven"
- [ ] **C** "I can't believe you made a hole in the roof!"
- [ ] **D** "You have good friends"

5 Who did the Pharisees say was the only one who could forgive sins?

- [ ] **A** them
- [ ] **B** God
- [ ] **C** the friends
- [ ] **D** Jesus

6 What does the Bible say Jesus knew?

- [ ] **A** what they were saying
- [ ] **B** what they were doing
- [ ] **C** what they were cooking
- [ ] **D** what they were thinking

7 What did Jesus say to the man?

- [ ] **A** "Get up and walk"
- [ ] **B** "Get up and walk home"
- [ ] **C** "Get up and dance"
- [ ] **D** "Get a move on"

8 Why did he tell the man to get up?

- [ ] **A** to show that the man was healed
- [ ] **B** to show he had authority to forgive sins
- [ ] **C** to show off
- [ ] **D** to show that God is love

9 What did the man NOT do?

- [ ] **A** get up
- [ ] **B** pick up his bed mat
- [ ] **C** go home thanking and praising God
- [ ] **D** rub his sore legs

10 What was the response of the people?

- [ ] **A** they clapped
- [ ] **B** they cheered
- [ ] **C** they praised God
- [ ] **D** they praised Jesus

QUEST V
KEEPER'S QUESTIONS

1 A crowd of people followed Jesus because they had seen him do what?

- A walk on water
- B heal lots of people
- C raise the dead
- D play the guitar

2 Jesus asked Philip how they would feed the people. Why?

- A to test him
- B to make him look silly
- C to give him a chance to work out how much money they had
- D because Philip was in charge of the money

3 What did Jesus tell his disciples to get the crowd to do?

- A line up
- B sit at tables
- C sit down
- D go to get themselves food

4 What did Jesus do when he was holding the bread?

- A he prayed very hard that God would do a miracle
- B he thanked God
- C he broke it into tiny pieces
- D he said the Lord's Prayer

5 When everyone realised that Jesus had done a miracle, what did they think of him?

- A he was very clever
- B he was the prophet who was to come into the world
- C he was a special messenger from God
- D he was amazing

6 What sort of food did Jesus say the people ought to work for?

- A food that can feed a crowd
- B food that God gives
- C food that makes you healthy
- D food that lasts for eternity

7 What did Jesus NOT say?

- A "I am the bread of life"
- B "No one who comes to me will ever be hungry"
- C "No one who comes to me will ever be thirsty"
- D "No one who comes to me will ever have manna from heaven"

8 Why did the people start grumbling?

- A because they were hungry
- B because they were thirsty
- C because Jesus said he was the bread of life
- D because Jesus said he had come down from heaven

9 What did Jesus say that everyone who has faith in him will have?

- A bread to eat
- B a blessed life
- C manna from heaven
- D eternal life

10 Where was Jesus when he taught these things?

- A the marketplace in Capernaum
- B in a boat on the lake
- C on a hill near Lake Galilee
- D the Jewish place of worship in Capernaum

QUEST QUIZ
KEEPER'S ANSWERS

QUEST I

1 Where did Jesus start teaching the people?
A on the shore of the lake

2 Why were the two boats empty?
D the fishermen were washing their nets

3 What did Jesus first ask Simon to do?
D push his boat a little way from the shore

4 When Jesus had finished talking to the people, what did he ask Simon to do?
B row out into deep water to catch some fish

5 Why was Simon not keen to go fishing?
D he had fished all night and not caught any fish

6 What happened when they let down their nets?
A they caught so many fish that their nets began ripping apart

7 What nearly happened when they put the fish into their and their friends' boat?
D the boats nearly sank

8 When he saw what happened, what did Simon realise about himself?
D he was a sinner

9 What did Jesus say to Simon?
C "Now you will be catching people"

10 What did the fishermen do once they were back on the shore?
B they pulled up their boats and left them to follow Jesus

QUEST II

1 In what town did this story take place?
A Capernaum

2 Who was sick?
B a Roman officer's servant

3 How sick was the sick person?
B they were very sick and about to die

4 When Jesus heard about the sick person, what did he do?
B he started to travel to the house where the sick person was

5 What did the officer do when he heard that Jesus was coming to his house?
D he sent a message to Jesus just to give the order to make the sick person well

6 Which command was NOT one which the officer gave as an example?
C "March!"

7 Why did the officer ask Jesus to give the order?
A he understood that Jesus had authority over sickness just as he had authority over soldiers

8 How did Jesus feel when the officer asked him to heal without visiting the house?
D surprised

9 What did Jesus say the officer had a lot of?
A faith

10 When was the servant healed?
D right away

QUEST III

1 What was the name of the man in charge of the Jewish meeting place or synagogue?
C Jairus

2 How old was the man's daughter?
B 12

3 What was wrong with her?
B she was dying

4 For how many years had the woman been bleeding?
B 12

5 What had she spent trying to get better?
B all her money

6 What happened when the woman touched Jesus' clothes?
A she was healed immediately

7 How did Jesus know someone had touched him?
D because he felt power go out from him

8 When Jesus heard that the little girl had died, what did he tell Jairus to have?
B faith

9 Who did NOT go into the house with Jesus?
C the people who were weeping outside

10 What did Jesus do as he told the girl to get up?
A he held her hand

QUEST IV

1 Where had the Pharisees and teachers of the Law NOT come from?
D Bethlehem

2 What did the men come carrying?
A a paralysed man on a mat

3 Why did they take the paralysed man on to the roof?!
C so they could make a hole and lower him into the room where Jesus was

4 When Jesus saw how much faith they had, what did he say to the man?
B "My friend, your sins are forgiven"

5 Who did the Pharisees say was the only one who could forgive sins?
B God

6 What does the Bible say Jesus knew?
D what they were thinking

7 What did Jesus say to the man?
B "Get up and walk home"

8 Why did he tell the man to get up?
B "To show he had authority to forgive sins"

9 What did the man NOT do?
D rub his sore legs

10 What was the response of the people?
C they praised God

QUEST V

1 A crowd of people followed Jesus because they had seen him do what?
B heal lots of people

2 Jesus asked Philip how they would feed the people. Why?
A to test him

3 What did Jesus tell his disciples to get the crowd to do?
C sit down

4 What did Jesus do when he was holding the bread?
B he thanked God

5 When everyone realised that Jesus had done a miracle, what did they think of him?
B he was the prophet who was to come into the world

6 What sort of food did Jesus say the people ought to work for?
D food that lasts for eternity

7 What did Jesus NOT say?
D "No one who comes to me will ever have manna from heaven"

8 Why did the people start grumbling?
D because Jesus said he had come down from heaven

9 What did Jesus say that everyone who has faith in him will have?
D eternal life

10 Where was Jesus when he taught these things?
D the Jewish place of worship in Capernaum

CLUB SONG WE ARE THE GUARDIANS OF ANCORA

Doug Horley and Mark Read

www.davidballmusicarranger.com

(v.2)
F   C   G   Pre-Chorus
by the po - wer of love. He has cho - sen you, (you!)
for e - ter - ni - ty.
F   C
he has cho - sen me, (me!) good news, to be
G
good news. I said: He has cho - sen you, (you!)
F   D
he has cho - sen me, to bring light in - to this world, come on!

PHOTOCOPIABLE PAGE

Whoa. Hey! Whoah.
(to v.2)
2. God's on-ly Son, Whoa.
Guar-di-ans of An-co-ra,
Bridge
Bring (bring) back (back) the light (light) to the ci-ty.
Bring (bring) back (back) the light (light) to the ci-ty.

To be chanted
G U A R D I A N S Guar-di-ans.
G5
Bring (bring) back (back) the light (light) to the ci-ty.
G U A R D I A N S Guar-di-ans.
F C
Bring (bring) back (back) the light (light) to the ci-ty.
D.S. al Coda
D
Drum fill
Bring-ing the light___back to the ci-ty. We are the
Coda
G5 F5 G5
Guar-di-ans___ of An - co - ra,

LEARN & REMEMBER SONG GOD IS LOVE

Nick and Becky Drake

♩ = 88 *Verse*

CCLI No. 6301004   Songs Of Fellowship Sheet Music

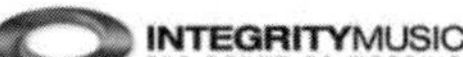

God, we love— You,— God, we love— You,
that is why— we— sing. God, we love— You,
God, we love— You,— God, we love— You.
You are why— we— sing. God— is
love, our— God is love.—